FROM MINDSET TO MARKET

THE BLUEPRINT FOR BUILDING A PROFITABLE BUSINESS

NEERAJ RAWAT

To my family, whose love and support have been the foundation of my success

Contents

Foreword — *vii*

Preface — *ix*

Acknowledgements — *xv*

Prologue — *xvii*

Introduction — *xix*

1. Understanding The Business Mindset — 1

2. Business Ideas And Opportunities — 16

3. Building A Business Plan — 35

4. Raising Capital And Financing Your Business — 57

5. Marketing And Sales — 87

6. Managing Your Business — 119

7. Overcoming Obstacles And Coping With Failure — 153

Summary Of The Book — 185

Foreword

As a successful business owner and entrepreneur, I know that building a strong and resilient mindset is essential for achieving your goals. In "From Mindset to Market," Neeraj Rawat shares a wealth of knowledge and insights that will help readers develop the mindset they need to succeed.

With clear and concise advice, Neeraj Rawat covers a range of topics, including market research, team building, negotiation skills, and more. The book is filled with real-world case studies and inspiring stories of entrepreneurial success that will motivate readers to pursue their dreams and overcome obstacles.

As a colleague and friend of the author, I can attest to their passion for helping others succeed. The tips and strategies outlined in this book are based on years of experience in the business world and are sure to help readers achieve their full potential.

"From Mindset to Market" is a must-read for anyone looking to start or grow a business. I highly recommend this book to all aspiring entrepreneurs and business owners.

Preface

What comes to mind after reading the sentence "Mindset"? It seems to be an ordinary word but has the power to change the vision of one's business perspective. If we talk about the history of business, the simple buying and selling of products started in the late 1700s. But there was no need to use a specific mindset as the meaning of business is limited to exchanging goods for goods. With the growth of technology, the world of business is also evolving, and to become a successful business, a mindset that is sharply dedicated to the business is needed. This book helps you from planning your business to achieving everything that a successful businessman wants. We are going to explore every aspect of business, from identifying the problem to finding the solution to the particular problem and tying everything together in a comprehensive plan.

When I was a young boy, I decided to start a lemonade stand with my friend. We were excited to make some money and have fun at the same time. However, when we set up our stand, we quickly realised that we had a problem. Nobody was stopping to buy our lemonade. At first, we were discouraged and considered giving up. But then we realised that we needed to think creatively and find a way to attract customers. We decided to make our lemonade stand more visible by adding colourful signs and decorations that would catch people's attention.

We also realised that we needed to differentiate ourselves from other lemonade stands in the area. So, we started experimenting with different flavours and began offering free samples to people who passed by. This helped us stand out and attract more customers. Over time, we continued to adapt and improve our lemonade stand by experimenting with different pricing strategies and finding ways to make it more efficient. By the end of the summer, we had made a significant profit and had learned a lot about entrepreneurship.

This experience taught me that in business, it's important to be creative and willing to adapt in order to succeed. This is the most common entrepreneurial example, which shows having a different mindset leads to a drastic change in one's business. Thinking outside the box in any business makes you different from other competitors and makes you successful. This mindset can be used to overcome any challenge and achieve your goals as an entrepreneur.

I recalled how my uncle used to teach me the essential characteristics of an effective businessman. One day I asked in curiosity how a successful person thinks. He replied to me with a great smile that excellence starts with questioning. A successful person does not think, "I can't make money." He always thinks, "How can I make money?" The difference in both sentences is that one is making a statement, while the other has the mindset to think about how he can make money. I conclude from his statement that the secret to being successful depends on one's mentality. While the unsuccessful person blames his fate, the other one thinks about how he can change the adverse situation by changing his point of view on the circumstances.

The first step in developing a successful business mindset is to identify the problem that needs to be solved. This may involve researching your target audience, understanding their needs, and identifying gaps in the market that you can fill. It could also involve identifying pain points or frustrations that customers have with existing products or services. Once you have identified the problem, you can begin to think about how to develop a solution that addresses it.

Once you have identified the problem, you need to develop a solution that addresses it effectively. This may involve developing a new product or service that meets a need in the marketplace or improving an existing one to make it more effective. Your solution should be innovative and provide value to your customer. This is where the importance of creativity comes in. To develop an effective solution, you need to think outside the box and come up with unique ideas.

To have a successful business, it is important to tie everything together into a comprehensive plan. This involves creating a business plan that outlines your goals, strategies, and tactics and maps out a clear path to success. It is also important to consider your finances, marketing and sales strategies, and the people you will need to make it all happen.

Developing a successful business mindset is a complex and challenging process, but it is essential for success as an entrepreneur. By identifying problems, developing innovative solutions, building a comprehensive business plan, raising capital, and implementing effective marketing and sales strategies, you can create a thriving business that stands out in the marketplace. This book will provide you with the knowledge and tools you need to develop a successful business mindset and achieve your entrepreneurial goal.

This book is the result of my studies in the world of business and my passion for helping others achieve success in their entrepreneurial journeys. I have worked with countless entrepreneurs, and I have seen firsthand the challenges and opportunities that come with building a successful business.

The purpose of this book is to provide a comprehensive guide to developing a successful business mindset. I believe that having the right mindset is critical to achieving success in business and that anyone can develop the skills and knowledge necessary to build a successful and fulfilling career. Whether you are just starting out on your entrepreneurial journey or looking to take your business to the next level, this book is designed to provide you with the tools and strategies you need to succeed.

Throughout the chapters that follow, I will share with you the key concepts and principles that underpin success in business, as well as practical advice and guidance on how to apply these concepts in your own career. From evaluating business ideas and opportunities to building a business plan, from raising capital and financing your business to marketing and sales, from managing your business to scaling and growth, this book covers a wide range of topics that are essential for building a successful business.

I have also included personal anecdotes and stories from successful entrepreneurs to provide you with real-world examples of the concepts and principles discussed in this book. My hope is that by reading this book, you will not only gain a deep understanding of what it takes to succeed in business but also the inspiration and motivation to pursue your own entrepreneurial dreams.

Thank you for choosing to read this book, and I wish you all the best in your entrepreneurial journey.

"Successful people do what unsuccessful people are not willing to do. Don't wish it were easier, wish you were better." -Jim rohn

Acknowledgements

I would like to express my deepest gratitude to all the people who have helped me in the writing and publishing of this book. First and foremost, I want to thank my family for their unwavering love and support throughout this journey. Their encouragement and belief in me have been my biggest motivators.

I also want to express my sincere thanks to my mentors and friends, who have generously shared their knowledge and expertise with me over the years. Their guidance has been invaluable in shaping my approach to entrepreneurship and business strategy.

To my editor and the team at the publishing house, thank you for your guidance, support, and expertise. Your insights and feedback have been invaluable in bringing this book to life.

Finally, I want to thank the readers who have taken the time to pick up this book. I hope that the insights and strategies presented here will help you build a strong and resilient business mindset and achieve your entrepreneurial dreams.

Prologue

It was just a few years ago that I found myself at a crossroads in my career. I knew that I wanted to start my own business and be my own boss. But as I began to explore this path, I realized that I lacked the mindset and skills necessary to succeed. It was then that I began to delve deep into the world of entrepreneurship and business strategy. Through countless hours of research, study, and trial and error, I slowly began to develop the mindset and strategies that would ultimately lead to my success.

Now, as I look back on my journey, I realize that the lessons I learned are valuable not just for me, but for anyone looking to build a successful business. It is my hope that this book will serve as a guide and a source of inspiration for entrepreneurs and business owners everywhere.

In the following pages, I share the insights and strategies that helped me build a successful business mindset. From market research to team building, negotiation skills to time management, I cover a wide range of topics that are essential for achieving your goals. So, whether you're just starting out or looking to take your business to the next level, I invite you to join me on this journey to building a successful business mindset.

Introduction

Welcome to this book on developing a successful business mindset. Whether you are an aspiring entrepreneur or an experienced business owner, this book is designed to help you develop the skills, knowledge, and mindset necessary for building a successful and fulfilling career.

The purpose of this book is to provide a comprehensive guide to the key concepts and principles that underpin success in business. We will explore a wide range of topics, including evaluating business ideas and opportunities, building a business plan, raising capital and financing your business, marketing and sales, managing your business, networking and collaboration, personal development, scaling and growth, overcoming obstacles and coping with failure, and future trends and innovation. Throughout this book, we will emphasize the importance of a growth mindset, resilience, and the ability to adapt to change. We will also discuss the critical role of self-awareness, emotional intelligence, and effective communication skills in building successful relationships and teams.

This book is intended for anyone who is interested in developing a successful business mindset, whether you are just starting out on your entrepreneurial journey or looking to take your business to the next level. By reading this book, you can expect to gain a deep understanding of the key principles and strategies for success in business, as well as practical advice and guidance on how to apply these concepts in your own career.

In the first chapter of the book, we will try to understand the business mindset and the characteristics of successful entrepreneurs. We will also explore the importance of having a growth mindset and how to develop a positive and proactive attitude towards risk and failure.

In the second chapter of this book, we will explore how to evaluate business ideas and opportunities, identify your unique skills and strengths, and explore topics like market trend research. This chapter also demonstrates how to implement any business idea from scratch and potential business ideas.

In the third chapter of this book, we will discuss how to develop a strong business plan. We will cover topics such as the importance of a well-structured business plan, competitive analysis, developing a sustainable business model, market strategy, financial planning, and operations planning.

In the fourth chapter, we will focus on the critical issue of raising capital and financing your business and explore the different options available to entrepreneurs, including venture capital, angel investing, crowdfunding, and traditional bank loans.

In the Fifth Chapter, we will cover topics related to marketing and sales, including KPIs, market and sales alignment, tools and techniques for alignment, market and sales analytics, case studies with real-life examples, and future trends and opportunities.

In the sixth chapter, we will explore the topics related to business management, including establishing a business management framework, financial management, cash flow management, HRM, operations management, marketing and sales management, risk management, and legal and regulatory compliance.

In the final chapter, we will explore strategies for coping with failure and overcoming obstacles. Types of Obstacles in Business: A Case Study of Successful Business

People Overcoming Obstacles and Coping with Failure, Impact of Obstacles and Failure on Business Success.

Thank you for joining me on this journey, and I look forward to exploring the world of business with you.

CHAPTER ONE

Understanding the Business Mindset

If you are an aspiring entrepreneur or business owner, understanding the business mindset is crucial. In this chapter, we will discuss what the business mindset is, its importance, and how to cultivate it.

I. How the business mindset looks like

The business mindset is a way of thinking that is focused on creating and growing a successful business. It involves a combination of entrepreneurial spirit, strategic thinking, and a willingness to take calculated risks. Those who possess the business mindset are often driven, persistent, and resilient in the face of challenges and setbacks.

The importance of the business mindset Having the right mindset is critical to the success of any business. Entrepreneurs who possess a business mindset are more likely to identify and pursue opportunities, develop innovative solutions, and stay focused on their goals. They are also better equipped to handle the inevitable challenges and failures that come with running a business. In short, the business mindset is essential for anyone who wants to create a successful, sustainable business.

Understanding a business mindset is not a difficult task if you observe events happening around you keenly. Let me illustrate the concept of the business mindset with a real-life observation. The story starts with a character named Nisha Rawat, who has always dreamed of starting her own business. She's passionate about opening a bakery and making beautiful and customised cakes for her customers. At first, she was hesitant and unsure of where to start.She knew that building a successful business would require a lot of hard work and dedication. But she also knew that she had to embrace the business mindset if she wanted to turn her dream into reality.

She started by doing some market research to determine if there was a demand for her new type of bakery in her local area. She talked to potential customers, asked for their feedback, and gathered data to help her make informed decisions. With a clear vision and a solid understanding of her market, Nisha started to take action. She created a business plan, secured funding, and began searching for a location to open her bakery.

She also knew that building a successful business would require resilience and the ability to embrace failure. When she encountered setbacks, she didn't give up. Instead, she learned from her mistakes, adapted her approach, and kept moving forward. She also focused on creating value for her customers and knew that if she wanted her business to succeed, she had to provide exceptional service and deliver real results for her clients. She invested in high-quality baking material and an atmosphere for reaching every client through social media.

As her business grew, she also focused on building strong relationships with her customers, employees, and other stakeholders. She listened to their feedback, addressed their concerns, and communicated openly and honestly.

Over the time, her business thrived, and her bakery became a go-to destination for customers in her local area as well as on social media platforms. Nisha's success was due in large part to her commitment to the business mindset—her ability to take calculated risks, embrace failure, and focus on value creation.

Nisha's story is a testament to the power of the business mindset. By embracing this way of thinking, entrepreneurs can turn their dreams into reality and build successful, sustainable businesses.

II. Cultivating the business mindset

Do you have ideas for a business, or maybe you are already an entrepreneur? Regardless of your current status, cultivating a business mindset is crucial to your success. Having the right mindset will enable you to navigate the many challenges that come with starting and running a business. Cultivating a business mindset is an ongoing process, but there are several steps you can take to get started. Here are some tips to help you develop a business mindset.

1. Set Goals

Goals provide a sense of direction, purpose, and focus for your business. Without clear goals, it's easy to get lost or overwhelmed, and it's difficult to measure progress and success.

When setting goals, it's important to make sure they are specific, measurable, and achievable. Here's a breakdown of what each of these criteria means:

Specific: Your goals should be clear and specific. Instead of setting a vague goal like "increase sales," make it more specific by stating "increase sales by 20% in the next quarter". A specific goal helps to provide focus and direction for your business.

Measurable: Your goals should be measurable, which means that you should be able to track progress and determine whether you have achieved the goal. In the example above, the goal is measurable because you can track sales and determine whether they have increased by 20% or not.

Achievable: Your goals should be achievable, which means that they are realistic and within your control. It's important to set challenging goals, but they should still be attainable. If your goal is too ambitious, it can be demotivating if you don't achieve it.

In addition to setting specific, measurable, and achievable goals, it's also important to create a plan to achieve them. Your plan should include specific action steps and deadlines to help you stay on track.

Here are some additional tips for setting goals:

Prioritize: Identify the most important goals for your business and prioritise them. Focus on achieving one or two goals at a time rather than spreading yourself too thin.

Write them down: Write your goals down and keep them visible. This will help you stay focused and motivated.

Review and adjust: Review your goals regularly and adjust them if necessary. As your business evolves, your goals may need to change to reflect new priorities and opportunities.

Celebrate successes: When you achieve a goal, take the time to celebrate your success. Recognizing your accomplishments can help keep you motivated and focused on achieving your next set of goals.

2. Be resilient

Being resilient is an important trait to cultivate when building a business mindset. It refers to the ability to bounce back from challenges and setbacks and to stay focused and motivated despite obstacles. Resilience doesn't mean that you won't experience difficulties or setbacks in your business journey. Instead, it means that you'll be better equipped to handle them and to keep moving forward. Here are some tips for building resilience:

Practice self-care: Running a business can be stressful, and it's important to take care of yourself both physically and mentally. This might include exercise, healthy eating, getting enough sleep, and taking breaks when you need them. By taking care of yourself, you'll be better equipped to handle the challenges that come your way.

Build a support network: Surround yourself with people who support and encourage you. This might include friends, family, mentors, or a business coach. Having a support network can help you stay motivated and provide a sounding board for ideas and challenges.

Set realistic goals: Setting realistic and achievable goals can help you stay motivated and build resilience. Instead of focusing on a big, audacious goal, break it down into smaller, more manageable steps. Celebrate each milestone along the way, and use each success as motivation to keep going.

Learn from failures: Failure is a natural part of the business journey, and it's important to learn from it. Instead of dwelling on mistakes or setbacks, try to understand what went wrong and how you can improve in the future. By learning from your failures, you can build resilience and develop the skills needed to succeed.

3. Take a calculated risk

A "calculated risk" is a decision to take an action that involves some degree of uncertainty or potential loss but has been carefully considered and evaluated.Here are some tips for taking calculated risks in business:

Do your research: Before making a decision, it's important to do your research and gather as much information as possible. This might include market research, financial analysis, or talking to industry experts. By gathering as much information as possible, you can make a more informed decision.

Evaluate the potential outcomes: consider the potential outcomes of the decision, both positive and negative. What is the potential upside, and what are the potential risks? By evaluating the potential outcomes, you can better understand the risks and make a more informed decision.

Consider the worst-case scenario: While it's important to focus on the potential upside, it's also important to consider the worst-case scenario. What is the potential loss if things don't go as planned? By considering the worst-case scenario, you can make a more informed decision about whether the potential risk is worth taking.

Start small: When taking a calculated risk, it's often a good idea to start small. This might mean testing a new product or service with a small group of customers or investing a small amount of money in a new venture. By starting small, you can minimise your risk while still testing the waters and gaining valuable experience.

Learn from your mistakes: Even when you take a calculated risk, there is always the potential for things to go wrong. When this happens, it's important to learn from your mistakes and use them as a learning experience. By learning from your mistakes, you can improve your decision-making skills and be better prepared for future risks.

By doing your research, evaluating the potential outcomes, considering the worst-case scenario, starting small, and learning from your mistakes, you can take risks in a more informed and strategic way. Remember that not every risk will pay off, but by taking calculated risks, you can learn and grow as an entrepreneur and achieve greater success in the long run.

4. Continuous learning in business

As an entrepreneur, it's important to stay up-to-date with the latest trends, technologies, and best practises in your industry. Continuous learning can help you stay competitive and adapt to changes in the market.Here are some tips for continuous learning in business:

Read widely: Read books, articles, and blogs related to your industry and related fields. This can help you stay up-to-date with the latest trends and best practices. You can also learn from the experiences of others and gain new insights into your business.

Attend industry events: Attend conferences, workshops, and other industry events. This can provide valuable networking opportunities and help you stay up-to-date with the latest trends and technologies in your field.

Take online courses: Online courses are a great way to learn new skills and gain knowledge in a flexible and convenient way. There are many platforms that offer online courses, such as Coursera, Udemy, and LinkedIn Learning.

Seek feedback: Feedback is an important part of learning and growing. Seek feedback from your customers, employees, and mentors. This can help you identify areas for improvement and make changes to your business.

Experimentation: Experimentation is an important part of learning and growth. Try new things, take risks, and don't be afraid to fail. By experimenting, you can learn from your mistakes and gain new insights into your business.

By reading widely, attending industry events, taking online courses, seeking feedback, and experimenting, you can stay competitive and adapt to changes in the market. Remember that learning is a lifelong process and that the more you learn, the more you can grow and succeed as an entrepreneur.

5. Networking in business

Networking is an important aspect of cultivating a business mindset. As an entrepreneur, building a strong network can help you build valuable relationships, find new customers, and gain access to resources that can help your business grow. Here are some tips for building and maintaining a strong network in business:

Attend industry events: Attending industry events is a great way to meet other entrepreneurs, industry experts, and potential customers. These events can provide valuable networking opportunities and help you stay up-to-date with the latest trends and technologies in your field.

Join professional organisations: Joining a professional organisation related to your industry can provide opportunities to meet like-minded people and learn from experts in your field. These organisations often have regular meetings, events, and online forums where you can connect with others.

Use social media: Social media platforms like LinkedIn, Twitter, and Instagram can be powerful tools for networking. You can use these platforms to connect with other entrepreneurs, share your own content, and engage with your followers.

Ask for introductions: If you know someone who might be able to help your business, don't be afraid to ask for an introduction. This can be a great way to build new relationships and expand your network.

Follow up: After meeting someone at an event or online, be sure to follow up with them. Send them an email or message, and keep the conversation going. This can help build a strong relationship over time.

By attending industry events, joining professional organisations, using social media, asking for introductions, and following up, you can build a strong network of relationships that can help your business grow. Remember that networking is a two-way street and that building strong relationships takes time and effort. By investing in your network, you can open up new opportunities and achieve greater success as an entrepreneur.

6. Be customer focused

As an entrepreneur, understanding and meeting the needs of your customers is key to building a successful business.

Here are some tips for being customer-focused in business:

Listen to your customers: Take the time to listen to your customers and understand their needs. This can be done through customer surveys, focus groups, or simply having conversations with them. By understanding what your customers want, you can tailor your products and services to meet their needs.

Provide excellent customer service: Providing excellent customer service is a key part of being customer-focused. Make sure that your employees are trained to handle customer inquiries, complaints, and feedback in a professional and helpful manner.

Anticipate customer needs: By understanding your customers' needs, you can anticipate what they might need in the future. This can help you develop new products and services that meet their changing needs.

Stay in touch with customers: Stay in touch with your customers through email newsletters, social media, or other means. This can help you stay top-of-mind and build strong relationships with your customers.

Act on customer feedback: When customers provide feedback, take it seriously and act on it. Use this feedback to improve your products and services and show your customers that you value their opinions.

By listening to your customers, providing excellent customer service, anticipating customer needs, staying in touch with customers, and acting on their feedback, you can build a strong and loyal customer base that will help your business grow. Remember that without customers, there is no business, so it's important to make sure that their needs are always front and centre.

7. Embrace change

Embracing change is a key aspect of cultivating a business mindset. As an entrepreneur, it's important to be adaptable and open to change in order to stay competitive in a rapidly evolving market. Here are some tips for embracing change in business:

Stay informed: Keep up-to-date with the latest trends and developments in your industry. This can help you anticipate changes and prepare for them in advance.

Be open to new ideas: Don't be afraid to try new things or think outside the box. Sometimes the most innovative and successful ideas come from taking risks and embracing change.

Learn from failures: Don't be discouraged by failures. Instead, use them as opportunities to learn and improve. By embracing change, you'll be more likely to try new things and take risks, which may lead to failures but also to new opportunities and successes.

Empower your employees: Encourage your employees to embrace change and be adaptable. This can help create a culture of innovation and continuous improvement within your business.

Stay flexible: As your business grows and evolves, be willing to adapt and change your strategies as needed. This can help you stay competitive and meet the changing needs of your customers.

By staying informed, being open to new ideas, learning from failures, empowering your employees, and remaining flexible, you can create a culture of innovation and adaptability that will help your business thrive. Remember that change is a constant in business, and the ability to embrace it can be the key to success in a rapidly evolving market.

III. How successful entrepreneurs look

Successful entrepreneurs are individuals who have the ability to identify a problem or an opportunity in the market and create a profitable solution. They are driven by their passion, determination, and vision to build something of their own and have a willingness to take risks.

Passion is a key characteristic of successful entrepreneurs. They are passionate about what they do and are motivated by their deep love and enthusiasm for their business. They are able to channel this passion into their work and use it to fuel their determination and drive. This passion is what separates successful entrepreneurs from those who are simply in it for the money.

Another important characteristic of successful entrepreneurs is their ability to innovate. They are constantly thinking of new and innovative ways to solve problems and create value. They are not content with the status quo and are always looking for ways to improve and disrupt their industry. This ability to think outside the box and create unique solutions is what sets successful entrepreneurs apart from their competitors.

Successful entrepreneurs are also visionary. They have a clear vision for their business and are able to communicate that vision to others. They have a long-term perspective and are focused on achieving their goals, even in the face of adversity. This vision helps them stay focused and motivated, even when things get tough.

Risk-taking is another important characteristic of successful entrepreneurs. They are not afraid to take risks and are willing to step outside of their comfort zone in order to achieve success. They are able to assess the risks and rewards of a particular decision and make a calculated decision based on the information available to them. This willingness to take risks is what allows successful entrepreneurs to achieve great things and create innovative solutions.

Successful entrepreneurs possess a number of key characteristics that set them apart from others. They are passionate, innovative, visionary, and risk-takers. These characteristics allow them to identify opportunities and create solutions that others have not thought of. By harnessing these traits and developing them further, anyone can become a successful entrepreneur and achieve their goals.

The importance of having a growth mindset

Having a growth mindset is very important for success in life, both personally and professionally. It enables individuals to see their potential for growth and development and believe that their abilities and intelligence can be developed and improved over time with effort and persistence. This is in contrast to a fixed mindset, where one believes that their abilities and intelligence are innate and cannot be changed.

One of the most important benefits of having a growth mindset is that it encourages personal growth. It helps individuals identify their strengths and weaknesses and believe that they can learn and improve in any area they choose. This can help individuals overcome challenges and setbacks and ultimately achieve their goals. With a growth mindset, individuals are not afraid to take on new challenges and try new things, as they believe that they can learn and grow from these experiences.

Another key benefit of having a growth mindset is that it increases resilience. Individuals with a growth mindset are able to view obstacles as opportunities to learn and grow rather than as insurmountable obstacles. They see setbacks as temporary and believe that they can overcome them with effort and persistence. This resilience can help individuals bounce back from setbacks and continue working towards their goals, even in the face of adversity.

Having a growth mindset can also boost motivation. Individuals with a growth mindset believe that their efforts can lead to growth and improvement, which can be highly motivating. They are willing to put in the effort and work hard, as they know that their efforts will pay off in the long run. This can help individuals stay focused on their goals and persist in the face of challenges and setbacks.

Having a growth mindset is crucial for personal and professional success. It encourages personal growth, increases resilience, and boosts motivation. By adopting a growth mindset, individuals can overcome challenges and setbacks, learn from their experiences, and ultimately achieve their goals.

Developing a positive and proactive attitude towards risk and failure

Developing a positive and proactive attitude towards risk and failure is crucial for business success. A positive attitude towards risk and failure means being willing to take calculated risks and being open to the possibility of failure.

One of the most important benefits of developing a positive and proactive attitude towards risk and failure is that it encourages innovation. It enables individuals to try new things and take risks without fear of failure. This can lead to new ideas, products, and services that can give businesses a competitive edge in the market.

Another key benefit of developing a positive and proactive attitude towards risk and failure is that it helps individuals learn from their mistakes. Failure can be a powerful teacher, and individuals who are willing to take risks and learn from their mistakes are more likely to succeed in the long run. By learning from their failures, individuals can refine their approach and strategies and ultimately become more successful.

Developing a positive and proactive attitude towards risk and failure also fosters resilience. It helps individuals bounce back from setbacks and continue working towards their goals, even in the face of failure. This resilience is critical in the fast-paced and competitive world of business, where setbacks are common.

CHAPTER TWO

Business ideas and opportunities

Idea! Idea! Idea! That's all it takes to build a strong platform for profitable business. When I was in college, I had a part-time job as a tutor. One day, a parent hired me to help her child with maths. The child was in 8th grade and struggling with algebra. As I worked with the students, I noticed that they were having difficulty visualising the concepts, which made it hard for them to understand the problems.

That's when I got an idea: what if I created a visual tool to help students understand maths concepts better? I started brainstorming and came up with the idea of a set of manipulatives that would allow students to physically move and manipulate numbers and variables, making abstract concepts more concrete.

I did some research and found that there was a gap in the market for this type of tool. There were a few existing products, but they were either too expensive or not versatile enough. So I decided to start my own business, creating and selling my own set of manipulatives.

I began by creating prototypes of the manipulatives using foam board and markers. I tested them with some of my tutoring students, and they loved them! I then worked on refining the design and figuring out how to mass-produce them.

After a few months of hard work, I launched my product on a popular e-commerce platform. The response was incredible! Within a few weeks, I had sold hundreds of sets of manipulatives to teachers and parents all over the country.

Today, my business is thriving. I have expanded my product line to include manipulatives for other maths concepts as well as for other subjects like science and language arts. I have also started selling directly to schools and have even partnered with a few school districts to provide manipulatives for their students.

Looking back, I never would have thought that my part-time job as a tutor would lead me to start my own business. But by paying attention to a real-life problem and coming up with a unique solution, I was able to turn a simple idea into a successful business opportunity.

Starting a business can be an exciting and rewarding experience, but it can also be daunting, especially if you're not sure what kind of business you want to start. In this chapter, we'll explore the process of generating business ideas, identifying opportunities, and evaluating their potential for success. We'll also provide some tips on how to refine your business ideas and find the right opportunity that aligns with your goals and values.

I. How to Generate a Good Business Idea

The first step in starting a business is to come up with a good business idea. There are several approaches you can take to generating a good business idea. Here are some detailed methods you can use:

One approach is to identify a problem and solve it. Start by identifying a common problem that people face in their everyday lives. This could be anything from a lack of time to prepare healthy meals to difficulty finding affordable housing or a need for a new type of service. Once you have identified the problem, brainstorm potential solutions. You may come up with a new product, service, or business model that can help solve the problem. From there, you can develop a business plan and begin to build your business around the solution you have created.

Another approach is to consider your passions and hobbies. Think about the things that you are passionate about or enjoy doing in your free time. This could be anything from playing sports to knitting to reading books. You may be able to turn one of these hobbies into a business idea. For example, if you are passionate about cooking, you could start a catering or meal delivery service. If you love knitting, you could start an online store that sells hand-knitted products. By building a business around something you love, you are more likely to be motivated and committed to making it successful.

Analyzing trends is another useful method for generating a good business idea. Stay up-to-date on industry trends and analyse what types of products or services are in high demand. This can help you identify a gap in the market and come up with a new business idea. For example, in recent years, there has been a growing interest in sustainable and environmentally friendly products. This has led to new business opportunities in areas such as recycling, renewable energy, and eco-friendly consumer products.

Looking for inefficiencies is another approach. Identify an existing business or industry that could be more efficient or cost-effective, and brainstorm ways to improve it. This can lead to new business ideas that are more efficient and cost-effective than existing options. For example, you could create a new software programme that automates a repetitive task or develop a new manufacturing process that reduces waste and improves productivity.

Considering the changing needs of society is another effective method for generating a good business idea. Think about the changing needs of society and how businesses can adapt to these changes. For example, in recent years, there has been a growing demand for flexible work arrangements and remote work options. This has led to new business opportunities in areas such as co-working spaces, virtual office services, and online collaboration tools.

Talking to others is a helpful method for generating new business ideas. Talk to friends, family, and colleagues about potential business ideas. Ask for their feedback and input, and see if they can offer any suggestions or ideas that you may not have considered. Getting feedback from others can help you refine your ideas and identify potential challenges or opportunities.

In conclusion, generating a good business idea requires creativity, research, and a deep understanding of the market and the needs of potential customers. By using the methods I have described, you can come up with a business idea that is unique, relevant, and has the potential to succeed. It's important to take the time to thoroughly research and evaluate your ideas before committing to a new business venture. With persistence and hard work, you can turn your business idea into a successful reality.

Identifying business opportunities

Once you have a business idea, it's important to evaluate its potential for success. Here are some key factors to consider when identifying opportunities:

Market Demand: Is there a market for your product or service? Who are your target customers, and what are their needs? Conduct market research to gather data on the size and potential of your target market.

Competition: Analyse the competitive landscape to see how many other businesses are offering similar products or services. Consider what sets your business apart from the competition and how you can differentiate your offerings.

Skills and Resources: Evaluate your own skills and resources. Do you have the necessary expertise to start and run the business? Do you have the financial resources or access to funding to get the business off the ground?

Regulatory Environment: Consider any regulatory or legal requirements that may apply to your business. Research the licences and permits you may need to obtain and any other legal obligations you'll need to comply with.

Problem-solving: Identify problems that you can solve with your business idea. This can include addressing issues with current products or services or identifying new problems that you can solve with your product or service.

Analyzing Customer Needs: Understanding the needs of your target audience is essential to identifying business opportunities. Consider factors such as demographics, location, income level, and lifestyle to identify the needs of your potential customers.

Refining the business idea

Once you've identified a business opportunity, it's time to refine your business idea. This includes developing a business plan that outlines your strategy for starting and growing your business. Here are some key elements to consider when refining your business idea:

Value Proposition: Clearly articulate the unique value that your product or service provides to customers. This should be the core of your business and a major focus of your marketing efforts.

Business Model: Develop a clear and concise business model that outlines how you'll make money. This should include revenue streams, cost structures, and key performance indicators.

Marketing Strategy: Identify your target market and develop a marketing strategy that will reach them effectively. This may include advertising, social media, content marketing, and other promotional tactics.

Financial Projections: Develop financial projections that outline your revenue and expense forecasts for the next few years. This should include a break-even analysis and cash flow projections.

Starting a business can be exciting and daunting at the same time. One of the most critical steps in this process is refining your business idea. Your business idea is the foundation upon which you will build your entire enterprise, so it's essential to make sure that it's viable and sustainable. The first step is to identify a problem that needs to be solved. The best businesses are those that solve a problem or fulfil a need that people have. Think about the pain points in your own life or the lives of people you know. Is there a problem that you could solve with a product or service? Start by brainstorming a list of potential problems you could solve, and then narrow it down to the one that you are most passionate about.

Once you have identified a problem, the next step is to research your market. It's essential to understand your target audience and whether there is a demand for your product or service. You need to know who your competitors are, what they offer, and how you can differentiate yourself from them. It's also crucial to analyse industry trends, regulations, and market projections to determine the potential for growth and profitability.

Another crucial factor to consider when refining your business idea is your unique selling proposition (USP). What sets your business apart from the competition? Your USP should be something that makes your product or service stand out and is difficult for competitors to replicate.

Finally, you need to evaluate the financial viability of your business idea. Determine how much it will cost to start and operate your business, including overhead expenses, marketing, and product development. Then, consider how much revenue you can realistically expect to generate and whether it's enough to cover your costs and generate a profit.

In Conclusion, Refining your business idea is an essential step in starting a successful business. By identifying a problem that needs to be solved, researching your market, developing a unique selling proposition, and evaluating the financial viability of your idea, you can create a solid foundation for your business and increase your chances of success.

Finding the right opportunity

Finally, it's important to find the right business opportunity that aligns with your goals and values. Here are some key questions to consider when evaluating a business opportunity:

1. Does the business align with your personal and professional goals?
2. Does the business align with your values?
3. Is there a clear path to profitability?
4. Do you have the necessary skills and resources to start and run the business?
5. Is the market large enough to support the business?
6. Is there a competitive advantage that you can leverage to differentiate your business?
7. What are the potential risks and challenges of starting and running the business?

Answering these questions can help you determine whether a business opportunity is a good fit for you. It's important to take the time to thoroughly evaluate each opportunity and consider all of the factors involved.

II. How to Implement Any Business Idea from Scratch

Conduct Market Research: The first step is to research the market demand for your business idea. Identify your target customers, understand their needs, and analyse your competitors.

Define Your Value Proposition: Determine your unique selling proposition, i.e., what sets your business apart from others in the market. Consider how you can add value to your customers and differentiate yourself from competitors.

Develop a Business Plan: Create a comprehensive business plan that includes your business model, marketing strategy, financial projections, and operational plan. A well-written business plan will help you stay focused, set goals, and track your progress.

Register your business: Register your business and obtain any necessary permits and licences. Choose an appropriate legal structure (such as an LLC, sole proprietorship, or partnership) and register with the relevant government agencies.

Securing Funding: Determine how much funding you need to start and run your business. Explore different funding options, such as loans, grants, or investors. Develop a financial plan that includes a detailed budget, income statement, and cash flow projection.

Build Your Team: Recruit a team of skilled and experienced professionals who can help you achieve your business goals. Consider hiring employees, contractors, or freelancers to perform various tasks.

Establish Your Brand: Develop a strong brand identity that represents your business values and personality. Create a logo, website, social media presence, and marketing materials that communicate your brand message effectively.

Launch Your Business: Launch your business and start promoting it to your target customers. Implement your marketing strategy, develop relationships with customers, and continually assess and improve your business operations.

Monitor Your Progress: Track your progress against your business plan and goals. Regularly review your financials, customer feedback, and industry trends to adjust your business strategy and remain competitive.

Continually innovate: Continue to innovate and grow your business by introducing new products or services, expanding your customer base, and staying ahead of your competition. Stay up-to-date with industry trends, technology, and customer needs to remain relevant and successful.

Factors contributing to the success of a business

Market Demand: There must be a market demand for your product or service. If there is no demand, then your business will not be successful.

Customer Focus: The success of your business is directly tied to the satisfaction of your customers. Focus on providing a high-quality product or service that meets the needs of your customers.

Unique Value Proposition: A unique value proposition is what sets your product or service apart from the competition. It is what makes your business stand out and attracts customers.

Financial Management: Managing your finances effectively is critical to the success of your business. This involves monitoring your cash flow, managing your expenses, and ensuring that your revenue exceeds your costs.

Teamwork: A successful business requires a strong team. Surround yourself with people who have the skills and expertise to help your business succeed.

III. Potential business ideas

1. Personalized Health and Wellness Coaching: With an increasing focus on health and wellness, there is a growing demand for personalised coaching services that help people achieve their health goals. A health and wellness coaching business could offer one-on-one coaching, group coaching, or online coaching sessions that focus on nutrition, exercise, stress reduction, and other aspects of a healthy lifestyle.

2. Eco-Friendly Cleaning Services: As consumers become more environmentally conscious, there is a growing demand for cleaning services that use eco-friendly products and methods. A cleaning service that uses non-toxic, biodegradable cleaning products and emphasises sustainable practices could be a great business idea for someone looking to start a service-based business.

3. Virtual Event Planning and Coordination: With the rise of remote work and virtual events, there is a growing demand for event planning and coordination services that can be done online. A virtual event planning and coordination business could help companies and individuals plan and execute virtual conferences, webinars, and other online events.

4. Pet Care Services: As pet ownership continues to grow, there is a growing demand for pet care services that help pet owners take care of their furry friends. A pet care business could offer services like dog walking, pet sitting, grooming, and training and could cater to both busy working professionals and pet owners who are travelling or on vacation.

5. Sustainable Fashion and Accessories: With growing concern about the environmental impact of fast fashion, there is a growing demand for sustainable fashion and accessories that use eco-friendly materials and ethical production methods. A sustainable fashion business could focus on creating clothing, accessories, and other products that are stylish, functional, and environmentally conscious.

6. Home-Based Childcare Services: With many parents juggling work and family responsibilities, there is a growing demand for quality childcare services that can be provided in a home-based setting. A home-based childcare business could offer services like babysitting, after-school care, and weekend care for children of various ages.

7. Online Language Instruction: With the growing importance of cross-cultural communication and the popularity of remote work and travel, there is a growing demand for online language instruction services. An online language instruction business could offer one-on-one or group classes in a variety of languages and cater to both individual learners and corporate clients.

8. Home Renovation and Restoration Services: With many homeowners looking to renovate or restore their homes, there is a growing demand for home renovation and restoration services that can help them achieve their goals. A home renovation and restoration business could offer services like remodelling, painting, flooring, and other interior and exterior renovation work.

9. Elderly Care Services: With an ageing population and a growing number of seniors requiring assistance with daily activities, there is a growing demand for elderly care services that can help seniors maintain their independence and quality of life. An elderly care business could offer services like in-home care, transportation, meal preparation, and companionship for seniors.

10. Personal Styling and Image Consulting: With the increasing emphasis on personal branding and image, there is a growing demand for personal styling and image consulting services that can help people look and feel their best. A personal styling and image consulting business could offer services like wardrobe assessments, personal shopping, and style consultations and cater to both individual clients and corporate clients.

11. Mobile App Development: Mobile apps are in high demand, with millions of people downloading and using them every day. You could create a business that specialises in developing mobile apps for various purposes. Your services could include developing apps for businesses, educational institutions, or non-profit organisations. You could also offer app design, development, and maintenance services.

12. Personal Fitness Training: With people becoming more health-conscious, personal fitness training is becoming a popular business idea. You could offer personalised fitness plans and training sessions for individuals or small groups. You could specialise in different areas, such as weight loss, strength training, or yoga. You could also offer virtual training sessions to clients who prefer to work out at home.

13. Digital Marketing and Advertising Agency: As more businesses move online, there is a growing demand for digital marketing and advertising services. You could create a business that specialises in providing digital marketing and advertising services to businesses of all sizes. Your services could include search engine optimization, social media marketing, pay-per-click advertising, and email marketing. You could also offer customised packages for clients based on their specific marketing goals and budgets.

14. Sustainable Fashion Brands: As consumers become more environmentally conscious, there is a growing demand for sustainable and ethical fashion brands. You could create a fashion brand that focuses on using eco-friendly materials and sustainable production methods. You could offer a range of clothing and accessories for men, women, and children and market your products as environmentally friendly and socially responsible.

15. Customized Meal Prep and Delivery Service: More and more people are looking for convenient, healthy meal options, and a customised meal prep and delivery service could be a great business idea. You could offer customised meal plans based on clients' dietary restrictions, preferences, and health goals. You could source high-quality, organic ingredients and offer delivery services to clients' homes or workplaces.

16. Organic Farm and CSA: With the increasing demand for organic and locally grown produce, you could create a business that specialises in organic farming and offers a Community Supported Agriculture (CSA) program. You could grow a variety of fruits, vegetables, and herbs and offer weekly or monthly deliveries to members of your CSA program.

17. Mobile Car Detailing Service: Many car owners are looking for convenient and affordable car detailing services. You could create a business that offers mobile car detailing services and comes to clients' homes or workplaces. Your services could include washing, waxing, and detailing both the interior and exterior of vehicles.

18. Online Tutoring Service: With the rise of e-learning and remote work, there is a growing demand for online tutoring services. You could create a business that offers personalised online tutoring services for students of all ages and levels. Your services could cover a wide range of subjects, from maths and science to writing and foreign languages.

19. Digital Product Development Service: If you have a background in software development or design, you could create a business that offers digital product development services to businesses of all sizes. Your services could include custom software development, mobile app development, and web design, with a focus on delivering high-quality, user-friendly products.

20. Sustainable Home Products: As consumers become more environmentally conscious, there is a growing demand for sustainable home products. You could create a business that specialises in producing and selling eco-friendly home products, such as cleaning supplies, kitchenware, and furniture. You could market your products as both sustainable and stylish, appealing to a wide range of customers.

21. Personal Styling and Wardrobe Consulting: Many people struggle with finding the right clothes and creating a cohesive wardrobe. You could create a business that offers personalised styling and wardrobe consulting services to clients of all ages and styles. Your services could include closet audits, personal shopping, and styling consultations.

22. Online artisan marketplace: If you have a passion for art and handmade goods, you could create an online marketplace that connects artisans with customers around the world. You could offer a range of unique, handmade items, such as pottery, jewellery, and textiles, and market your platform as a source of one-of-a-kind, sustainable, and ethical products.

23. Mobile App Marketing and Optimization: With the increasing number of mobile apps available, you could create a business that specialises in marketing and optimising mobile apps for businesses of all sizes. Your services could include app store optimization, social media marketing, and influencer outreach to help your clients reach a wider audience and improve user engagement.

24. Senior Care Services: As the population ages, there is a growing demand for senior care services. You could create a business that offers a range of senior care services, including home care, transportation, meal delivery, and companionship. You could also offer specialised services, such as Alzheimer's and dementia care.

25. Social Media Management: With the growing importance of social media for businesses, you could create a business that offers social media management services to help businesses increase their online presence and engage with customers. Your services could include social media strategy development, content creation, community management, and analytics reporting.

26. Online Marketplace for Local Products: If you have a passion for supporting local businesses and artisans, you could create an online marketplace that connects local producers with customers in your area. You could offer a range of locally sourced products, such as food, beverages, and handmade goods, and market your platform as a source of high-quality, sustainable, and community-minded products.

27. Travel Planning Service: As people start to travel again, you could create a business that offers personalised travel planning services to help people plan and book their dream vacations. Your services could include itinerary planning, hotel and transportation booking, and travel insurance, with a focus on delivering unique and unforgettable travel experiences.

28. Virtual Therapy and Counseling: With the increasing need for mental health support, you could create a business that offers virtual therapy and counselling services to clients. You could offer a range of services, such as individual therapy, couples therapy, and group sessions, to help clients manage their mental health and well-being.

IV. Conclusion

Developing a business idea and identifying business opportunities are fundamental steps in starting a successful business. A business idea is the foundation of any business and should be based on a market need or problem. It should also have the potential to generate revenue and create value for its customers. Identifying business opportunities involves conducting thorough market research, understanding customer needs, and analysing the competition. Market research is essential to understanding the market landscape and identifying gaps or opportunities. It helps to analyse industry trends, customer needs, and the competition. By doing so, you can assess whether your business idea has the potential to succeed and gain a competitive advantage.

It is equally important to identify customer needs and preferences. Understanding your target audience and their needs can help you tailor your product or service to better meet their demands. By analysing customer demographics, location, income levels, and lifestyles, you can develop a product or service that appeals to your target audience.

Another key factor to consider is competition. Analyzing your competitors can help you differentiate your product or service and identify unique selling points. By identifying your competitors' strengths and weaknesses, you can develop a strategy that sets you apart from the competition and attracts customers.

Once you have identified a business opportunity, it is important to focus on factors that contribute to the success of your business. These include market demand, customer satisfaction, a unique value proposition, financial management, and teamwork.

Market demand is critical to the success of any business. If there is no demand for your product or service, your business will not be successful. Therefore, it is essential to conduct market research and identify a market need that aligns with your business idea.

Customer satisfaction is also important to the success of your business. Your customers are the lifeblood of your business, and it is essential to provide them with high-quality products or services that meet their needs. A unique value proposition sets your product or service apart from the competition. It is what makes your business stand out and attracts customers. By developing a unique value proposition, you can differentiate your business from the competition and gain a competitive advantage.

Financial management is critical to the success of your business. Managing your finances effectively involves monitoring your cash flow, managing your expenses, and ensuring that your revenue exceeds your costs. By managing your finances effectively, you can ensure the financial stability and longevity of your business.

Finally, teamwork is a critical factor in the success of your business. Surrounding yourself with people who have the skills and expertise to help your business succeed is essential. By building a strong team, you can delegate tasks and responsibilities, work efficiently, and achieve your business goals.

Starting a business can be challenging, but it can also be rewarding. With careful planning, hard work, and perseverance, you can turn your business idea into a profitable venture that provides value to your customers and contributes to your success. It is essential to be adaptable and willing to make changes as you learn more about your business and the market. By focusing on market demand, customer satisfaction, a unique value proposition, financial management, and teamwork, you can develop a successful business that provides value to your customers and contributes to your success.

CHAPTER THREE

Building a Business Plan

I. Introduction

Business planning is an essential process for entrepreneurs and business owners who want to start or grow their businesses. It involves creating a roadmap that outlines the goals, strategies, and action plans needed to achieve success. A business plan typically includes an overview of the company's products or services, market analysis, marketing and sales strategies, financial projections, and management practices.

At its core, business planning is about taking a step back to look at the big picture and identify what needs to be done to achieve the desired outcomes. It's a process that helps entrepreneurs and business owners think through their ideas, test assumptions, and make informed decisions. It's also an important tool for securing funding or investment, as investors and lenders want to see a clear and comprehensive plan for the business.

Business planning doesn't have to be complicated or overwhelming. In fact, it can be a fun and creative process that allows entrepreneurs to explore new ideas and opportunities. The key is to approach it with an open mind and a willingness to learn and adapt.

Importance of Business Planning

Let me take some real-world examples that will demonstrate how business planning is important for the growth of any company.

Uber is a company that transformed the transportation industry by creating a ride-sharing platform that allows drivers to connect with passengers through a mobile app. Founded in 2009, the company has grown rapidly and expanded into over 700 cities worldwide. In 2019, the company had over 100 million active users and a market capitalization of over $100 billion.

One of the key reasons why Uber has been so successful is its business planning process. From the beginning, the company had a clear vision of its goals and objectives, and it developed a comprehensive business plan to achieve them. The plan included a detailed analysis of the ride-sharing market, competitor analysis, financial projections, and marketing and sales strategies.

The first reason why business planning is important is that it helps entrepreneurs and business owners define their goals and objectives. In the case of Uber, the company's primary goal was to disrupt the transportation industry by creating a more efficient and convenient way for people to travel. By defining this goal, the company was able to focus its resources and efforts on developing a product that would meet the needs of its target market.

The second reason why business planning is important is that it helps entrepreneurs and business owners identify potential challenges and opportunities. In the case of Uber, the company's business plan included a comprehensive analysis of the ride-sharing market and competitor analysis. This analysis helped the company identify potential challenges and opportunities, such as the regulatory and legal issues that arise in the transportation industry, as well as the potential for expansion into new markets.

The third reason why business planning is important is that it helps entrepreneurs and business owners make informed decisions. In the case of Uber, the company's business plan included financial projections, which helped the company make decisions about funding, investment, and growth. By having a clear understanding of its financial position, the company was able to make informed decisions about its future.

The fourth reason why business planning is important is that it can help entrepreneurs and business owners secure funding or investment. In the case of Uber, the company's business plan was critical to securing funding from investors. The plan included detailed financial projections, marketing strategies, and an overview of the company's operations, all of which helped investors understand the potential for growth and profitability.

Business planning is an important process that helps entrepreneurs and business owners define their goals and objectives, identify potential challenges and opportunities, make informed decisions, and secure funding or investment. The real-world example of Uber demonstrates the importance of business planning in achieving success and growth in a competitive market. By developing a comprehensive business plan, Uber was able to identify and address potential challenges and opportunities, make informed decisions, and secure funding from investors. As such, any entrepreneur or business owner who wants to succeed and grow their business must understand the importance of business planning and invest time and resources into developing a solid plan that will guide their actions and decisions.

The second example is "Apple." In 2007, Steve Jobs introduced the first iPhone, revolutionising the smartphone industry. However, the iPhone wasn't just the result of a new and innovative product idea; it was also the product of meticulous planning and preparation.

In the years leading up to the launch of the iPhone, Apple had been working on the development of the device, but it wasn't until Jobs and his team began to develop a comprehensive business plan that the iPhone really began to take shape. They recognised that the success of the iPhone was dependent on more than just the technology; it needed to be marketed and positioned in the right way to attract customers.

The business plan for the iPhone included a detailed analysis of the market, competitors, and potential sales channels. It also included financial projections and an overview of the manufacturing and supply chain logistics needed to bring the product to market. By developing this plan, Apple was able to identify potential challenges and opportunities and create a strategy for launching and promoting the iPhone.

When the iPhone was finally launched in 2007, it was an immediate success. Apple had a clear understanding of the market, had created a product that was both innovative and user-friendly, and had developed a comprehensive marketing and sales strategy to promote the product. The result was a product that transformed the smartphone industry and created a new revenue stream for Apple.

This example demonstrates the importance of business planning in achieving success and growth. Apple's business plan for the iPhone helped them identify potential challenges and opportunities, make informed decisions, and develop a strategy for launching and promoting the product. Without this plan, the iPhone may not have been as successful or may have failed entirely. It shows that business planning is not just an optional step in starting or growing a business but a critical process that can make the difference between success and failure.

II. Benefits of Having a Solid Business Plan

A solid business plan is an essential tool for any entrepreneur or business owner, regardless of the size or type of their business. It is a written document that outlines the company's goals, strategies, and tactics for achieving them. A well-crafted business plan is a roadmap for success, and it offers numerous benefits that can help businesses achieve their objectives.

1. Clarity of Vision and Direction: One of the primary benefits of having a solid business plan is the clarity of vision and direction it provides. A business plan serves as a guide for entrepreneurs to stay focused on their goals and objectives. It outlines the company's mission, goals, and strategies for achieving them. This clarity of vision and direction helps entrepreneurs make informed decisions about how to allocate resources and prioritise tasks to achieve their goals.

2. Access to Financing and Investors: Another significant benefit of a solid business plan is its potential to attract investors and secure financing. A well-crafted business plan is a tool that entrepreneurs can use to convince investors and lenders to provide funding. It shows that the entrepreneur has a clear understanding of the business's potential and how they plan to achieve their goals. The plan includes financial projections, marketing strategies, and a competitive analysis, which help investors understand the business's potential and the likelihood of its success.

3. Identifies Potential Problems: A solid business plan includes a thorough analysis of the market, industry, competition, and potential challenges. This analysis helps entrepreneurs identify potential problems and address them before they arise. By identifying potential problems in advance, entrepreneurs can take steps to mitigate them, reducing their impact on the business's operations and profitability.

4. Provides a Clear Path to Growth: A solid business plan also provides a clear path to growth. It outlines the steps entrepreneurs need to take to grow their business, such as expanding their product line, entering new markets, or hiring additional staff. By having a roadmap for growth, entrepreneurs can stay focused on their goals and avoid distractions that may lead them off course.

5. Helps to Monitor Progress: A business plan is a living document that should be updated regularly as the business grows and changes. By tracking progress against the plan, entrepreneurs can identify areas where they are falling short of their goals and make adjustments to their strategy to get back on track. This monitoring helps entrepreneurs stay accountable to their goals and ensure that they are making progress towards their vision.

A solid business plan is critical for the success of any business. It provides clarity of vision and direction, access to financing and investors, identifies potential problems, provides a clear path to growth, and helps monitor progress. A well-crafted business plan is a powerful tool that entrepreneurs can use to achieve their goals and take their business to the next level.

III. What is the executive summary of a business plan?

An executive summary is a brief, high-level overview of a business plan or proposal that provides a snapshot of the key information and highlights the most important aspects of the plan. It's typically the first section of a business plan, but it's written last, after the rest of the plan has been completed.

The purpose of the executive summary is to provide the reader with a clear and concise overview of the entire plan or proposal, so they can quickly understand the main points and determine if they want to read the rest of the document. The executive summary should be well-written, engaging, and persuasive, and should highlight the most important aspects of the plan, such as the business's unique value proposition, market opportunity, and financial projections.

The length of the executive summary can vary, but it's generally no more than two pages. It should include the following key elements:

1. **Business concept:** A brief introduction to the business, including the products or services offered, the target market, and the competitive landscape.

2. **Market opportunity:** A summary of the market opportunity, including market size, growth trends, and customer needs.

3. Unique value proposition: a clear statement of the business's unique value proposition, including the key benefits the business offers to customers.

4. Marketing and sales strategy: An overview of the marketing and sales strategies that the business will use to reach and acquire customers

5. Financial projections: A high-level summary of the financial projections, including revenue, expenses, and profit margins

6.Management team: A brief introduction to the management team, including their relevant experience and qualifications

The executive summary should be written in a clear and concise style, with a focus on communicating the most important information in an engaging and persuasive way. It should be free of jargon and technical language, and it should be written with the target audience in mind, whether it's potential investors, lenders, or other stakeholders.

In summary, the executive summary is a crucial component of a business plan or proposal, as it provides a snapshot of the most important aspects of the plan and allows the reader to quickly understand the key points. A well-written executive summary can help persuade investors or lenders to take a closer look at the plan and can ultimately help to secure the funding or support needed to launch or grow a successful business.

IV. Company Description

The company description is an overview of the business, including its history, legal structure, and location. This section should provide a brief introduction to the company and include information such as the company's name, location, and legal structure (e.g., LLC, corporation, etc.). It should also highlight any key milestones or accomplishments that the company has achieved and describe the company's overall mission and values.

The company description should include the following information:

1. Description of the Business and its Products or Services: This section should provide a more detailed description of the business and the products or services it offers. It should include information about the target market, the unique value proposition of the business, and any competitive advantages it may have. This section should also outline the specific products or services offered by the business and describe their features, benefits, and pricing.

2. Company History and Mission Statement: The company history section should provide a brief overview of the company's history, including any key milestones or accomplishments. This section should also include the company's mission statement, which is a clear and concise statement of the company's overall purpose and goals. The mission statement should be brief and memorable and clearly communicate the company's core values and vision.

3. Market Analysis: The market analysis section should provide a detailed overview of the industry and market in which the business operates. This section should include information about the size and growth rate of the market, key trends and drivers, and the competitive landscape. It should also include a detailed analysis of the target market, including customer demographics, needs, and preferences, as well as an analysis of the competition and their strengths and weaknesses.

Overall, these sections of the business plan provide a clear and concise overview of the business and its market and help lay the foundation for the rest of the plan. A well-written and comprehensive company description, description of the business and its products or services, company history and mission statement, and market analysis can help to build credibility and demonstrate the potential of the business to potential investors, lenders, or other stakeholders.

Industry Analysis

Industry analysis is a crucial process for any business that wants to understand its operating environment and position itself for success. The analysis provides a detailed understanding of the industry in which a business operates, including its current state, future prospects, and major trends. This analysis is important as it helps businesses identify opportunities and challenges in their industry and develop strategies to capitalise on the former and overcome the latter.

The following are the key components of industry analysis:

1. Industry Definition: The first step in industry analysis is to define the industry. This involves identifying the product or service that the industry provides, the key players, and the regulatory framework that governs the industry. This step is important because it helps the business identify its competitors and understand the market demand for its products or services.

2. Market Size and Growth Rate: The second step is to determine the market size and growth rate of the industry. This involves analysing the demand for the product or service, identifying the target market and the size of the market, and forecasting the growth rate of the industry over the next few years. This step is important because it helps the business identify the potential for growth and market saturation and adjust its strategies accordingly.

3. Industry Trends: The third step is to analyse industry trends. This involves identifying the major trends that are shaping the industry, such as technological innovations, changes in consumer behaviour, and shifts in government policy. This step is important because it helps the business identify potential opportunities and challenges and develop strategies to capitalise on the former and overcome the latter.

4. Industry Structure: The fourth step is to analyse the industry structure. This involves identifying the key players in the industry, their market share, and their competitive advantages. This step is important because it helps the business identify potential threats from competitors and develop strategies to overcome them.

5. Porter's Five Forces: One popular framework for analysing industry structure is Porter's Five Forces model. The five forces include the threat of new entrants, the bargaining power of buyers, the bargaining power of suppliers, the threat of substitute products or services, and the intensity of competitive rivalry. This step is important because it helps the business identify the overall competitive intensity of the industry and develop strategies to compete effectively.

6. Key Success Factors: The final step is to identify the key success factors for the industry. This involves identifying the critical factors that determine success in the industry, such as technology, distribution channels, brand recognition, and customer service. This step is important because it helps the business focus on the areas that are most critical to success and develop strategies to excel in those areas.

Industry analysis is an important process for any business that wants to understand its operating environment and position itself for success. The analysis provides a detailed understanding of the industry in which a business operates, including its current state, future prospects, and major trends. By analysing the market size and growth rate, industry trends, industry structure, Porter's Five Forces, and key success factors, businesses can identify opportunities and challenges in their industry and develop strategies to capitalise on the former and overcome the latter.

V. Market Strategy

A market strategy is a comprehensive plan that a business develops to identify and address the needs of its target market, differentiate itself from competitors, and create sustainable growth. An effective market strategy is critical for any business to succeed, regardless of its size, industry, or location. In this essay, we will delve into the details of marketing strategy, including its components, the key steps in developing one, and the benefits it provides to businesses.

A market strategy typically includes several components that work together to achieve a common goal. The most critical components are:

1. Target Market Identification: The first step in developing a marketing strategy is identifying the target market. This involves understanding the customers' needs, preferences, and behaviours, as well as their demographics, location, and purchasing power. The target market is the group of customers who are most likely to purchase the company's products or services.

2. Competitive Analysis: The next step is to analyse the competition. This involves identifying the strengths and weaknesses of the company's competitors, their market share, pricing strategies, and marketing tactics. This information helps the company to differentiate itself from its competitors and create a unique selling proposition (USP).

3. Value Proposition: A "value proposition" is a statement that describes the benefits that the company's products or services provide to the customers. It answers the question, "Why should customers buy from us?" The value proposition should be clear, concise, and compelling.

4. Marketing Mix: The marketing mix is a set of tactics that the company uses to promote its products or services. It includes the four Ps: product, price, place, and promotion. The company must develop a product that meets the needs of the target market, price it appropriately, distribute it through the right channels, and promote it effectively.

5.Sales and Distribution Channels: The company must decide on the best sales and distribution channels for its products or services. This may include direct sales, online sales, retail sales, or a combination of these channels. The company must also consider how it will deliver its products or services to customers and provide after-sales support.

6. Marketing Budget: The marketing budget is the amount of money that the company allocates to its marketing activities. The budget should be realistic and based on the company's financial resources and marketing goals.

Developing a market strategy requires careful planning, research, and analysis. The following steps can help businesses develop an effective market strategy:

1. Define Business Goals: The first step is to define the company's goals. This may include increasing sales, expanding into new markets, or launching new products or services. The goals should be specific, measurable, achievable, relevant, and time-bound (SMART).

2. Conduct Market Research: The next step is to conduct market research to gather information about the target market, the competition, and the industry. This may involve analysing customer surveys, conducting focus groups, or using other research methods.

3. Identify Target Market: Based on the market research, the company can identify its target market. This involves segmenting the market based on demographics, psychographics, and behaviour.

4. Develop a Unique Selling Proposition: The next step is to develop a unique selling proposition (USP) that differentiates the company from its competitors. The USP should be based on the company's strengths and address the customers' needs and preferences.

5. Develop a Marketing Mix: The company must develop a marketing mix that includes product, price, place, and promotion. This involves designing a product that meets the target market's needs, pricing it appropriately, identifying the right distribution channels, and promoting it through various marketing tactics.

6. Allocate Marketing Budget: The company must allocate its marketing budget based on its marketing goals, the target market, and the marketing mix. The budget should be realistic, and the company should track its marketing expenses to ensure that it stays within budget.

7. Implement and monitor: After developing the marketing strategy, the company must implement it and monitor its effectiveness. This involves executing the marketing tactics, measuring the results, and making adjustments as needed.

Benefits of a Market Strategy

A well-developed market strategy offers several benefits to businesses, including:

1. Increased Sales: A market strategy helps businesses identify and target the customers who are most likely to purchase their products or services, which can lead to increased sales.

2. Competitive Advantage: A market strategy helps businesses differentiate themselves from their competitors by developing a unique selling proposition and marketing mix that meet the customers' needs and preferences.

3. Improved Customer Relationships: A market strategy helps businesses understand their customers' needs and preferences, which can lead to improved customer relationships and increased customer loyalty.

4. Cost-Effective Marketing: A market strategy helps businesses allocate their marketing budget more effectively, which can lead to cost-effective marketing and a better return on investment.

5. Sustainable Growth: A market strategy helps businesses develop a plan for sustainable growth by identifying new markets, new products, and new marketing tactics.

In conclusion, a market strategy is a critical component of any business's success. It helps businesses identify their target market, differentiate themselves from their competitors, and create sustainable growth. By following the steps outlined in this essay and including the critical components of a marketing strategy, businesses can develop a comprehensive and effective marketing strategy that meets their marketing goals and helps them succeed in today's competitive marketplace.

VI. Financial Planning

Financial planning in business is the process of identifying and organising a company's financial resources to achieve its objectives. It involves creating a roadmap to achieve short-term and long-term financial goals, analysing financial risks and opportunities, and determining the resources needed to achieve those goals.

Financial planning is a critical component of business management as it helps businesses achieve their financial objectives, such as improving profitability, minimising financial risks, and maximising the return on investment. Here are the key steps involved in financial planning in business:

1. Establish financial objectives: The first step in financial planning is to establish the company's financial objectives. These objectives may include increasing revenue, reducing costs, expanding market share, or improving profitability. Objectives should be SMART (specific, measurable, achievable, realistic, and time-bound) to ensure they can be realistically achieved.

2. Conduct a financial analysis: After establishing the financial objectives, a financial analysis should be conducted to assess the company's current financial situation. This includes reviewing the company's income statement, balance sheet, and cash flow statement. The analysis will help the business identify financial strengths and weaknesses and areas for improvement.

3. Develop a financial plan: Based on the financial analysis, the company can then develop a financial plan that outlines the steps needed to achieve the financial objectives. This may involve setting financial targets, identifying the resources needed, and creating a budget.

4. Implement the financial plan: Once the financial plan is developed, it must be put into action. This may involve allocating resources, creating financial reports, and monitoring progress towards financial goals. It's important to review the financial plan regularly and make adjustments as needed.

5. Monitor and evaluate performance: Finally, the company must monitor and evaluate its financial performance. This involves tracking financial metrics, such as revenue, expenses, and profits, and comparing actual performance to the financial plan. This will help the business identify areas for improvement and make the necessary adjustments.

In summary, financial planning is a critical process for businesses to achieve their financial goals. By establishing financial objectives, conducting a financial analysis, developing a financial plan, implementing the plan, and monitoring performance, businesses can ensure they are on the right path to financial success.

Operation Planning

An operations plan is an essential part of business planning that outlines the strategies and tactics a business will use to achieve its goals and objectives. It is an actionable plan that defines the steps a company will take to deliver its products and services, manage its resources, and optimise its processes to meet its customers' needs. In this article, we will provide a detailed explanation of an operations plan in business planning.

An operations plan focuses on the day-to-day activities of a business and how they will be executed. The plan outlines the procedures, policies, and responsibilities of each department within the company and how they will work together to achieve the company's objectives. It also defines the resources required to carry out these activities, such as personnel, equipment, and facilities, and the timeline for their completion.

The purpose of an operations plan is to ensure that a company can deliver high-quality products or services to its customers consistently, efficiently, and cost-effectively. It also ensures that the company can effectively manage its resources to achieve its objectives while minimising risks and optimising its operations. A well-written operations plan can provide a roadmap for the company to follow, allowing it to anticipate and avoid potential issues and risks.

A typical operations plan includes the following components:

1. Operational Objectives: These are the goals that the company aims to achieve through its operations. They should be specific, measurable, achievable, relevant, and time-bound (SMART). Examples of operational objectives include improving product quality, reducing manufacturing costs, increasing production capacity, and enhancing customer satisfaction.

2. Operational Strategy: This is the overall approach that the company will use to achieve its operational objectives. The company's operations strategy should align with its overall business strategy and be consistent with its mission, vision, and values. It should also take into account the company's strengths and weaknesses, as well as external factors such as market trends, competition, and regulations.

3. Key Performance Indicators (KPIs): These are the metrics that the company will use to measure its performance and progress towards its operational objectives. Examples of KPIs include product quality, production efficiency, customer satisfaction, and employee productivity. The KPIs should be specific, measurable, relevant, and time-bound (SMART) and should be regularly monitored and reviewed.

4. Operating Procedures: These are the standard procedures and processes that the company will use to carry out its operations. They should be documented and communicated to all employees involved in the operations. Operating procedures should cover all aspects of the operations, including product design, manufacturing, quality control, customer service, and supply chain management.

5. Resource Requirements: These are the resources that the company will need to carry out its operations. They include personnel, equipment, facilities, and materials. The resource requirements should be carefully evaluated to ensure that they are sufficient to meet the operational objectives while minimising costs and risks.

6.Timeline and Milestones: This is the timeline for carrying out the operations plan and achieving the operational objectives. The timeline should be realistic and take into account external factors such as market trends, competition, and regulations. It should also include milestones that mark significant achievements along the way.

Once the operations plan is developed, it should be reviewed regularly to ensure that it remains relevant and effective. The plan should be flexible enough to adapt to changes in the market, customer needs, and technology. The company should also regularly monitor and review its KPIs to identify areas for improvement and make necessary adjustments to the operation plan.

An operations plan is a crucial part of business planning that outlines the strategies and tactics a company will use to achieve its operational objectives. It focuses on the day-to-day activities of the company and how they will be executed. A well-written operations plan can provide a roadmap for the company to follow, allowing it to anticipate and avoid potential problems.

VII. Conclusion

Building a business plan is an essential step for any entrepreneur or business owner looking to start or grow a business. A business plan serves as a roadmap for the future, outlining the goals and strategies for the business as well as the steps needed to achieve them.

The process of building a business plan requires careful research, analysis, and planning. It involves identifying the target market, analysing the competition, and developing a unique value proposition that sets the business apart from its competitors. It also involves developing a clear and concise executive summary, outlining the company's mission and values, and providing a detailed financial analysis that includes projections for revenue, expenses, and cash flow.

While the process of building a business plan can be time-consuming and challenging, it is also a valuable opportunity for entrepreneurs to reflect on their business idea, test assumptions, and refine their strategy. By taking the time to research and analyse the market and competition, entrepreneurs can gain a deeper understanding of their target customers and identify new opportunities for growth and expansion.

A well-written and comprehensive business plan can also be an effective tool for securing funding or support from investors, lenders, or other stakeholders. By presenting a clear and compelling case for the business, entrepreneurs can demonstrate the potential for growth and profitability and provide assurance that they have a solid plan in place for achieving their goals.

It's important to note that a business plan is not a static document. As the business evolves and grows, the plan will need to be updated and revised to reflect changes in the market, the competition, and the overall business environment. Regular review and analysis of the business plan can help entrepreneurs stay on track and adapt to new challenges and opportunities.

In addition to the practical benefits of building a business plan, the process can also be a valuable learning experience for entrepreneurs. By examining their business idea from multiple angles, testing assumptions, and considering different scenarios and outcomes, entrepreneurs can develop a deeper understanding of their business and the market in which they operate.

CHAPTER FOUR

Raising Capital and Financing Your Business

I. Introduction

Capital raising and financing are essential parts of running and growing a successful business. Capital is the money that a business needs to invest in its operations, purchase equipment and inventory, hire staff, and market its products or services. In most cases, businesses need to raise capital externally to fund their operations, and this is where capital raising and financing come into play. This process involves acquiring funding from various sources, including investors, lenders, and grants. In this chapter, we will explore what capital raising and financing are, the different financing options available to businesses, and the importance of having a solid business plan in place when seeking funding. We will also discuss the pros and cons of different financing options and how to negotiate effectively with lenders and investors to secure favourable terms and conditions. Whether you are a startup or an established business looking to expand, understanding the capital-raising and financing process is crucial to your success.

Different types of financing

Equity financing, debt financing, and crowdfunding are three different types of financing options that businesses can use to raise capital. Each of these financing options has its own advantages and disadvantages, and it is important for businesses to understand them before choosing which one to use.

1.Equity Financing:

Equity financing involves selling a portion of the ownership of a company in exchange for funding. The investors who provide the funding become shareholders of the company and share in its profits and losses. The two most common types of equity financing are provided by angel investors and venture capital firms.

Common equity finance products include angel investment, venture capital, and private equity.

a) Angel Investors: Angel investors are typically high-net-worth individuals who invest their own money in early-stage startups. These investors are often experienced entrepreneurs or industry experts who provide not only funding but also mentorship, strategic guidance, and valuable connections. Angel investors are usually the first outside investors to support a startup, and they typically invest between $25,000 and $500,000, although investments can range higher.

Angel investors are looking for companies with high growth potential and a strong management team. They tend to invest in companies in industries where they have expertise or a personal interest. Angel investors typically expect a return on their investment within five to seven years, and they usually receive equity in the company in exchange for their investment.

b) Venture Capitalists: Venture capitalists (VCs) are professional investors who provide funding to early-stage and growth-stage companies. VCs typically invest larger amounts of money than angel investors, often in the range of $1 million to $10 million or more. They invest in companies that have demonstrated some level of traction, such as revenue growth, customer acquisition, or product development. VCs provide not only funding but also strategic guidance and operational support.

VCs typically invest in companies that have the potential to become market leaders in their industry. They look for companies with a strong management team, a clear path to profitability, and a scalable business model. VCs typically expect a high return on their investment within five to ten years, and they often take an active role in the management of the company. VCs usually receive equity in the company in exchange for their investment, and they may also require board seats or other governance rights.

c) Private Equity Firms: Private equity (PE) firms are professional investors who provide funding to mature companies that are already generating revenue and profits. PE firms typically invest larger amounts of money than VCs, often in the range of $10 million to $100 million or more. They invest in companies that have demonstrated strong financial performance, and they aim to help these companies grow and improve their operations.

PE firms typically invest in companies that are undervalued or have growth potential, and they use their expertise to improve the company's performance and profitability. PE firms usually take a controlling stake in the company in exchange for their investment, and they may use leverage (i.e., borrowed money) to finance the investment. PE firms typically expect a high return on their investment within three to seven years, and they may exit the investment by selling the company to another buyer, taking the company public, or by other means.

Advantages of Equity Financing

One of the biggest advantages of equity financing is that the business does not have to repay the funding. Unlike loans, equity financing does not accrue interest, and there are no fixed repayment terms. This can be particularly beneficial for startups or early-stage companies that may not have the cash flow to make regular loan payments.

Another advantage of equity financing is that it can provide access to valuable expertise and resources. Angel investors and venture capital firms often have extensive networks and can provide guidance and connections to help the business grow.

Disadvantages of Equity Financing

One of the biggest disadvantages of equity financing is that it can be expensive. Giving up a portion of the ownership of the company means that the profits are also shared with the investors, which can be costly in the long run.

Another disadvantage of equity financing is that it can lead to a loss of control. When investors own a portion of the company, they also have a say in the company's decision-making process. This can be challenging for entrepreneurs who are used to making all the decisions for their business.

2.Debt Financing:

Debt financing refers to the practice of borrowing money from a lender, which must be repaid with interest over time. The most common forms of debt financing are bank loans, lines of credit, and alternative financing options. Each of these financing options has its own unique advantages and disadvantages, and choosing the right one depends on the specific needs and circumstances of the borrower.

a) Bank Loans: Bank loans are a traditional form of debt financing in which a borrower obtains a lump sum of money from a bank or other financial institution. The borrower then repays the loan, typically with interest, over a predetermined period of time. Bank loans can be secured or unsecured. Secured loans require collateral, such as real estate, equipment, or inventory, while unsecured loans do not.

Bank loans are often used for large, one-time expenses, such as purchasing a piece of equipment or financing a major project. They are also useful for businesses that have a strong credit history and can demonstrate their ability to repay the loan. Bank loans generally have fixed interest rates and regular payments, which can make it easier for borrowers to budget and plan for the repayment of the loan.

b) Lines of credit: Lines of credit are a type of revolving credit in which a borrower has access to a predetermined amount of money from a lender. The borrower can draw on the line of credit as needed, up to the limit of the credit line, and only pays interest on the amount borrowed. Lines of credit are often used for short-term working capital needs, such as purchasing inventory or covering payroll during a slow period.

Lines of credit can be secured or unsecured, and they can have variable or fixed interest rates. Because lines of credit are revolving, they can provide flexibility and help businesses manage cash flow fluctuations.

c) Alternative Financing Options: In recent years, a variety of alternative financing options have emerged, providing businesses with additional options for obtaining capital. These options include crowdfunding, peer-to-peer lending, and invoice financing.

Alternative financing options can be useful for businesses that have difficulty obtaining traditional bank loans or lines of credit. They may offer more flexible repayment terms, lower interest rates, or faster access to capital. However, these options can also have higher fees and may be riskier for lenders, which can lead to higher interest rates or more stringent borrowing requirements.

Advantages of Debt Financing:

One of the biggest advantages of debt financing is that the borrower retains full ownership of the company. Unlike equity financing, debt financing does not require the business to give up any ownership or control.

Another advantage of debt financing is that the interest on the loan is tax-deductible. This can be particularly beneficial for businesses that have a high tax liability.

Disadvantages of Debt Financing:

One of the biggest disadvantages of debt financing is that the borrower is required to make regular payments on the loan, regardless of the business's cash flow. This can be challenging for businesses that are experiencing financial difficulties or that have irregular cash flows.

Another disadvantage of debt financing is that it can be difficult to obtain for startups and early-stage businesses. Lenders often require collateral and a strong credit history, which can be challenging for new businesses.

3. Crowdfunding:

Crowdfunding is a newer form of financing that has become increasingly popular in recent years. Crowdfunding involves raising small amounts of money from a large number of people, typically through an online platform. There are two main types of crowdfunding: reward-based crowdfunding and equity crowdfunding.

Reward-based crowdfunding involves offering rewards, such as products or services, to people who contribute to the campaign. This type of crowdfunding is often used by startups to raise funds for a specific project or product.

Equity crowdfunding involves selling ownership shares in the company to the investors who contribute to the campaign. This type of crowdfunding is similar to equity financing, but it is open to a larger pool of investors.

Advantages of crowdsourcing:

One of the biggest advantages of crowdfunding is that it provides access to a large pool of potential investors. This can be particularly beneficial for startups and early-stage businesses that may not have access to traditional financing options.

Another advantage of crowdfunding is that it can help businesses test their ideas and get feedback from potential customers. By engaging with their supporters, businesses can get valuable insights into what their customers want and need.

Disadvantages of crowdsourcing:

One of the biggest disadvantages of crowdfunding is that it can be time-consuming and challenging to set up and manage a campaign. Businesses need to have a clear and compelling message to attract supporters, and they also need to be able to manage the logistics of fulfilling rewards or managing shareholders.

Another disadvantage of crowdfunding is that it can be competitive. There are many businesses competing for funding on crowdfunding platforms, so it can be difficult to stand out from the crowd and get the attention of potential investors.

II. Preparing for fundraising

Preparing for fundraising is a critical step for any startup or early-stage business that is looking to secure external funding. A well-prepared pitch deck, financial projections, and key metrics are essential components of a successful fundraising strategy. In this article, we will explore these components in detail and explain what investors look for in each of them.

1. Building a Pitch Deck

A "pitch deck" is a visual presentation that outlines a business idea or concept for potential investors. It is typically a slide deck consisting of 10–15 slides that provides an overview of the company, its product or service, market opportunity, competitive landscape, and team. The purpose of a pitch deck is to convey the key aspects of a business in a concise and compelling way, with the ultimate goal of convincing investors to fund the venture.

When building a pitch deck, it's important to keep in mind that investors receive a large volume of pitches, so your deck needs to stand out. Here are some tips on how to make your pitch deck more compelling:

a) Start with a strong opening: The first few slides of your pitch deck are critical to capturing the attention of investors. Start with a compelling opening that sets the tone for the rest of the presentation.

b) Tell a story: A pitch deck is not just a collection of slides. It should tell a story that connects with the investor and builds a narrative around the business opportunity.

c) Keep it simple: Avoid complex jargon and focus on communicating your message in a clear and concise manner.

d) Include visuals: Use visuals to illustrate key points and make the presentation more engaging.

e) Highlight the team: Investors invest in people as much as they invest in ideas. Be sure to highlight the experience and expertise of your team.

f) Be honest: Investors appreciate transparency and honesty. Be upfront about the challenges and risks associated with the business opportunity.

2.Financial Projections

Financial projections are an important component of any pitch deck. They provide a roadmap for the financial success of the business and help investors understand the potential return on their investment. Financial projections typically include a projected income statement, balance sheet, and cash flow statement.

When building financial projections, it's important to be realistic and conservative. Here are some tips on how to prepare financial projections that investors will find compelling:

a) Start with revenue: Investors are most interested in the revenue potential of a business. Start your projections with a detailed revenue model that outlines the sources of revenue and the pricing strategy.

b) Be conservative: Investors are wary of overly optimistic projections. Be realistic in your projections and include a range of scenarios to demonstrate the potential upside and downside.

c) Include key assumptions: Be clear about the assumptions that underpin your projections. This will help investors understand the risks and uncertainties associated with the business opportunity.

d) Use visuals: Use graphs and charts to make your financial projections more engaging and easy to understand.

e) Update your projections regularly: Financial projections are not set in stone. Update them regularly to reflect changes in the business and the market.

3.Key Metrics

Key metrics are the indicators that investors use to track the progress and success of a business. They provide a way to measure the performance of the business and determine whether it is on track to achieve its goals. Key metrics vary depending on the business and the industry, but some common examples include revenue growth, customer acquisition cost, churn rate, and lifetime value of a customer.

When presenting key metrics to investors, it's important to be transparent and provide context. Here are some tips on how to present key metrics in a way that investors will find compelling:

a) Focus on the metrics that matter: Don't overwhelm investors with too many metrics. Focus on the ones that are most important to the business and demonstrate progress towards key goals.

b) Be transparent: Be honest about the challenges and risks associated with the metrics. Investors appreciate transparency and want to understand the potential risks and uncertainties associated with the business.

c) Provide context: Don't just present the metrics in isolation. Provide context by comparing them to industry benchmarks or previous periods.

e) Demonstrate a plan for improvement: Investors want to see that the business is actively working to improve its key metrics. Be sure to demonstrate a clear plan for improvement and highlight any progress made to date.

f) Use visuals: Use charts and graphs to make the metrics more engaging and easier to understand.

Fundraising process

The fundraising process is important for any business looking to scale up or launch a new venture. It involves identifying potential investors, presenting a compelling pitch, and negotiating the terms of the deal. In this article, we will provide a detailed explanation of the fundraising process and offer some tips to help you navigate it successfully.

1. Finding investors

The first step in the fundraising process is to identify potential investors. There are several ways to go about this, including:

a) Networking: This involves reaching out to your personal and professional networks and asking for referrals to potential investors. You can also attend industry events, conferences, and trade shows to meet potential investors.

b) Online platforms: There are several online platforms, such as AngelList and Gust, that connect entrepreneurs with potential investors. These platforms allow you to create a profile, upload your business plan and pitch deck, and connect with investors who are interested in your industry.

c) Incubators and accelerators: These organisations provide mentorship, resources, and funding to startups in exchange for equity. They can also introduce you to potential investors and help you refine your pitch.

When identifying potential investors, it's important to consider their investment criteria. For example, some investors may focus on early-stage startups, while others may only invest in established businesses. Some investors may have a specific industry or geographic focus, while others may be more flexible. By understanding an investor's investment criteria, you can tailor your pitch to their interests and increase your chances of success.

2. Pitching to Investors

Once you have identified potential investors, the next step is to pitch your business to them. A pitch typically involves a presentation that outlines your business model, market opportunity, team, and financial projections. Here are some tips to help you create a compelling pitch:

a) Keep it concise: Investors are busy and don't have a lot of time to spend on each pitch. Your pitch should be no longer than 10–15 slides and focus on the key points of your business.

b) Tell a story: Your pitch should tell a compelling story about your business and why it matters. Use anecdotes and examples to illustrate your points and engage your audience.

c) Focus on the problem you are solving: Investors want to know that your business is addressing a real need in the market. Be clear about the problem you are solving and how your solution is unique.

d) Highlight your team: Investors invest in people as much as they invest in ideas. Be sure to highlight the experience and expertise of your team and explain why they are well-suited to execute your business plan.

e) Be realistic about financial projections: While investors want to see that you have a plan for making money, they also want to see that your projections are realistic. Don't inflate your numbers or make unrealistic assumptions about your market.

3. Negotiating a Deal

If an investor is interested in your business, the next step is to negotiate the terms of the deal. This typically involves discussions around the amount of funding, the equity stake the investor will receive, and any other terms and conditions of the investment. Here are some tips to help you negotiate a favourable deal:

a) Know your value: Before entering into negotiations, it's important to have a clear understanding of the value of your business. This includes your revenue, profit margins, and any other assets you have. This information will help you determine a fair valuation for your business and negotiate a favourable deal.

b) Be flexible: While it's important to have a clear idea of what you want out of the deal, it's also important to be flexible. Negotiations involve give and take, and you may need to make concessions in order to reach an agreement.

c) Get everything in writing: Once you have reached an agreement, be sure to get all of the terms in writing. This includes the amount of funding, the equity stake, and any other terms and conditions of the investment. Having a written agreement can help prevent misunderstandings down the line and ensure that both parties are clear about their obligations.

d) Seek legal advice: It's a good idea to have a lawyer review the investment agreement before you sign it. A lawyer can help you understand the terms of the agreement and ensure that your interests are protected.

e) Build a good relationship: Remember that fundraising is not just about securing funding; it's also about building a relationship with your investors. Be responsive to their questions and concerns, and keep them informed about the progress of your business. Building a good relationship with your investors can lead to future opportunities for funding and support.

III. Valuing your company

Valuing a company is a process of determining the financial worth of the company, which can help attract potential investors and negotiate better terms. In this article, we will discuss the steps involved in valuing a company and negotiating terms with investors.

Step 1: Understanding the Purpose of Valuation

Before you start valuing your company, it is essential to understand the purpose of valuation. Valuation is not a one-size-fits-all process, and the approach can vary depending on the reason for the valuation. There can be multiple reasons for valuing a company, including:

- Selling the company
- Mergers and acquisitions
- Bringing in investors
- Estate planning

- Tax purposes
- Litigation

Understanding the purpose of valuation can help you determine the appropriate valuation method and the factors that will be given more weightage during the valuation process.

Step 2: Select the Valuation Method

There are several methods for valuing a company, and each has its own advantages and limitations. The commonly used methods are:

a) Asset-Based Valuation: This method values the company based on its net assets. It considers the value of all the assets, including cash, investments, inventory, and property, minus the liabilities.

b) Income-Based Valuation: This method considers the future cash flow of the company and determines its present value using a discount rate. It is suitable for companies with a stable and predictable income stream.

c) Market-Based Valuation: This method values the company by comparing it to similar companies in the same industry. It considers metrics like price-to-earnings ratio, price-to-sales ratio, and price-to-book ratio.

It is essential to choose the appropriate valuation method based on the purpose of the valuation, the industry, and company-specific factors.

Step 3: Gather financial information

To determine the value of a company, you need to gather its financial information, including historical financial statements, tax returns, projected financial statements, and other relevant data. This information helps in determining the company's financial health, growth prospects, and potential risks.

Step 4: Conduct a Comparative Analysis

Once you have gathered the financial information, it is time to conduct a comparative analysis. This involves analysing the financial information of similar companies in the same industry to get a benchmark valuation. The comparative analysis helps in determining whether the company is undervalued or overvalued in comparison to its peers.

Step 5: Calculate the Valuation

Based on the chosen valuation method, financial information, and comparative analysis, you can now calculate the valuation of the company. This step requires a sound understanding of financial modelling and analysis.

Step 6: Negotiate Terms with Investors

Once you have determined the value of the company, you can start negotiating terms with potential investors. The negotiation process can be tricky, and it is essential to approach it in a friendly and professional manner. Here are some tips for negotiating terms with investors:

a) Understand the Investor's Goals: It is essential to understand the investor's goals and expectations before starting the negotiation process. This can help you tailor your pitch and negotiate more effectively.

b) Be Prepared: Before entering into negotiations, make sure you have a clear understanding of the company's financials, growth prospects, and potential risks. This information can help you defend your valuation and negotiate better terms.

c) Be Flexible: Negotiation is a give-and-take process, and it is essential to be flexible during the negotiation process. Be open to compromises and try to find a win-win solution.

d) Build a rapport: Building a good rapport with the investor can go a long way towards establishing a positive and productive relationship. Be respectful, transparent, and communicate clearly throughout the negotiation process.

Closing the deal

Closing the deal refers to the final stage of a negotiation or sales process in which the parties involved finalise the agreement they have been discussing and agree on the terms and conditions that will govern their relationship going forward. This stage is crucial because it marks the transition from negotiation to execution and ensures that all parties are clear on their respective rights and obligations.

The process of closing the deal typically involves several steps, which may vary depending on the nature of the agreement and the parties involved. However, the following are some common steps that are involved in closing a deal:

1. Reviewing the terms of the agreement: At this stage, the parties review the terms of the agreement they have negotiated and ensure that they are in line with their expectations. This includes reviewing the terms of payment, delivery, warranties, and any other conditions that were agreed upon.

2. Signing the contract: Once the terms of the agreement have been reviewed and agreed upon, the parties sign the contract. This signifies their commitment to the terms of the agreement and creates a binding legal document that can be enforced in case of any disputes.

3. Fulfilling any outstanding conditions: Depending on the nature of the agreement, there may be certain conditions that need to be fulfilled before the agreement can be finalized. For example, if the agreement involves the sale of a property, the buyer may need to obtain financing or conduct a final inspection of the property before closing the deal.

4. Transferring ownership: In cases where the agreement involves the transfer of ownership, the parties may need to take steps to transfer ownership from the seller to the buyer. This may involve signing over the title to the property, transferring shares in a company, or any other relevant documentation.

5. Making payment: Once all conditions have been met and ownership has been transferred, the buyer is typically required to make payment to the seller in accordance with the terms of the agreement. This may involve making a lump-sum payment or making payments over a period of time.

III. Grow your business using fundraising

Using funds raised to grow your business can be a crucial step towards achieving your business goals. Here are some ways to use capital to grow your business effectively:

1. Expand your product or service offerings: One way to use the funds raised is to expand your product or service offerings. You can use the capital to develop new products or services or to improve existing ones. This can help you attract more customers and increase revenue.

2. Increase marketing efforts: Another way to use the funds raised is to increase your marketing efforts. This can include digital marketing, social media advertising, print advertising, and other forms of marketing. Increased marketing can help you reach more potential customers and build brand awareness.

3. Hire new employees: If your business is growing, you may need to hire new employees to keep up with demand. You can use the funds raised to hire new staff, which can help you expand your operations and increase revenue.

4. Upgrade equipment or technology: upgrading your equipment or technology can also be a good use of the funds raised. This can help you improve efficiency, reduce costs, and increase productivity. Upgrading technology can also help you stay competitive in your industry.

5.Open new locations: If your business is successful, you may want to consider opening new locations. You can use the funds raised to open new stores, offices, or warehouses in different locations. This can help you reach new customers and increase revenue.

6. Reduce debt: If you have debt, using the funds raised to pay it off can be a smart move. Reducing debt can improve your financial position and help you qualify for better financing in the future.

7. Invest in research and development: Finally, you can use the funds raised to invest in research and development. This can help you stay ahead of the competition and develop new products or services that can drive growth in the future.

Managing Investor Relationships

Managing investor relationships is a critical aspect of running any successful business, particularly those seeking external financing or support. Maintaining positive relationships with investors involves effective communication, timely reporting, and responsiveness to their needs and concerns.

Here are some key points to keep in mind when managing investor relationships:

1. Effective communication: Communication is essential to maintaining positive relationships with investors. Business owners should be open and transparent with investors about their company's operations, finances, and goals. Investors should be informed of any significant developments, challenges, or opportunities that may impact the business. Communication can be done through regular updates via email, phone, or in-person meetings.

2. Timely reporting: reporting is a critical component of investor relations. Investors expect regular financial reports, which provide them with insights into the company's performance. Reporting should be timely, accurate, and comprehensive, providing investors with the information they need to make informed decisions. Financial reports can include financial statements, budgets, and cash flow projections.

3. Maintaining positive relationships: Positive relationships with investors are built over time through trust, honesty, and mutual respect. It's important to demonstrate a willingness to listen to investors' concerns, answer their questions, and provide them with the information they need. Business owners should also be prepared to address any issues or concerns that investors may have.

4. Addressing concerns: It's important to address any concerns that investors may have promptly. This includes addressing any issues raised in the financial reports, answering questions, and addressing any concerns about the business's performance. Investors need to feel that their concerns are being taken seriously and that the business is committed to resolving any issues.

5. Demonstrating a long-term vision: Investors are often interested in the long-term potential of a business. It's important to demonstrate a clear vision for the future of the company and how it will achieve its goals. This includes sharing the business's plans for growth, expansion, and potential new opportunities.

Understanding Risk

When creating a business plan, it's important to identify and address potential risks that may impact your business's success. Investors will want to know that you have a plan in place to mitigate these risks and that you understand the potential challenges your business may face. Here are some steps you can take to identify and address risks in your business plan:

1. Conduct a risk assessment: Start by identifying potential risks that may impact your business, including market risks, operational risks, financial risks, and regulatory risks. Consider both internal and external factors that may impact your business's success.

2. Prioritize risks: Once you've identified potential risks, prioritise them based on their likelihood of occurrence and potential impact on your business. This will help you focus on the most critical risks when developing your risk mitigation plan.

3. Develop a risk mitigation plan: For each prioritised risk, develop a plan to mitigate the risk or minimise its impact. This may include strategies such as diversifying your customer base, implementing backup systems, or obtaining insurance.

4. Address risks in your business plan: Your business plan should include a section that outlines the potential risks your business may face and how you plan to mitigate these risks. Be transparent about the potential challenges your business may face and demonstrate that you have a plan in place to address them.

5.Update your risk assessment and mitigation plan regularly: Risks can change over time, so it's important to regularly review and update your risk assessment and mitigation plan as your business evolves. This will help you stay prepared for potential challenges and demonstrate to investors that you are proactive in addressing risks.

By taking these steps to identify and address risks in your business plan, you can demonstrate to investors that you have a realistic understanding of the potential challenges your business may face and that you are taking steps to mitigate these risks and ensure long-term success.

IV. The due diligence process

Due diligence is the process of assessing a company's financial, legal, operational, and strategic risks before making an investment decision. It is a critical step in the investment process that helps investors make informed decisions by identifying potential problems and evaluating the company's strengths and weaknesses. Here are the key things to expect during the due diligence process and how to prepare for them:

1. Financial due diligence:

During this process, the investor will evaluate your company's financial statements, cash flow, revenue, expenses, assets, and liabilities. The investor will want to see how profitable the business is, how sustainable the revenue streams are, and what expenses the company incurs. To prepare for this, you should make sure your financial statements are accurate and up-to-date. You should also have a detailed understanding of your company's financials and be prepared to answer any questions the investor may have.

2. Legal due diligence:

The investor will want to review all legal documents, contracts, and agreements that your company has entered into. This includes employee contracts, customer contracts, and vendor agreements. They will also look at any pending or past lawsuits and legal disputes. To prepare for this, you should gather all the necessary legal documents and contracts and ensure they are up-to-date and properly executed. It is also important to disclose any legal disputes or potential liabilities upfront.

3. Operational due diligence:

The investor will want to know how your company operates, including your management team, organisational structure, and operational processes. They will also look at your sales and marketing strategy, customer service procedures, and manufacturing or production processes. To prepare for this, you should have a clear and concise understanding of your company's operations, including your team's roles and responsibilities, your standard operating procedures, and your sales and marketing strategy.

4.Strategic due diligence:

The investor will want to know your company's short- and long-term goals, vision, and strategic plan. They will want to know how you plan to scale the business and what your competitive advantage is. To prepare for this, you should have a clear and well-defined strategic plan that outlines your company's goals and objectives, including how you plan to achieve them.

5.Data room:

During the due diligence process, you will need to create a virtual data room where investors can access all the information they need. This data room should include all the financial, legal, operational, and strategic documents that the investor will need to evaluate your company. To prepare for this, you should organise all your company's documents in a clear and concise way that makes it easy for the investor to find the information they need.

Tax implications of financing

Financing can have significant tax implications. In general, the way you finance your business can affect your tax situation in terms of the deductions you can claim, the tax treatment of interest and principal payments, and the potential tax consequences of any profits or losses.

To minimise your tax liability, it's important to work with a tax professional who can help you navigate the complex tax laws and regulations. Here are some steps to take when working with a tax professional:

1. **Understand your business structure:** Different types of businesses have different tax requirements, so it's important to understand your business structure and how it impacts your tax situation.

2. **Keep accurate records:** Good record-keeping is essential for minimising your tax liability. Make sure you keep track of all your income and expenses, including receipts, invoices, and bank statements.

3.**Communicate regularly with your tax professional:** Your tax professional can provide valuable guidance on how to structure your financing to minimise your tax liability. Make sure you communicate regularly with your tax professional and keep them informed of any changes to your business.

4.Plan ahead: Tax planning is essential for minimising your tax liability. Work with your tax professional to develop a tax strategy that takes into account your business goals and objectives.

Negotiating with Investors

Negotiating with investors is a crucial part of raising capital for your business. Effective negotiation skills are essential to ensure that you get the best deal possible for your company while also establishing a strong relationship with your investors. Here are some strategies for negotiating with investors and finding common ground:

1. **Research and preparation:** Before starting any negotiation, it's essential to do your research and prepare. This includes understanding your company's value proposition, your competition, your financial projections, and your goals for raising capital. Understanding your investor's background, investment style, and past investments is also important. This will help you build a stronger negotiation strategy and provide a solid foundation for discussing the terms of the investment.

2. **Be clear about your goals and priorities:** It's crucial to understand your goals and priorities before entering into a negotiation. This includes the amount of capital you need, the equity you're willing to give up, and the terms of the investment. Being clear about your goals and priorities will help you make informed decisions during the negotiation and avoid any misunderstandings or confusion.

3. **Build relationships:** Building strong relationships with your investors is important for long-term success.

During the negotiation, it's important to focus on building trust and establishing a good working relationship. This includes listening to their concerns, showing empathy, and being transparent about your plans and goals. Investors are more likely to invest in a company that they believe in and that they feel has the potential for long-term success.

4. Find common ground: Negotiations are about finding common ground and reaching an agreement that benefits both parties. This means being flexible and willing to compromise on certain terms while still ensuring that your company's needs are met. It's important to understand the investor's needs and goals and find a solution that works for both parties. This may involve finding creative solutions that meet both parties' objectives.

5.Keep the big picture in mind: During negotiations, it's important to keep the big picture in mind. This means understanding the long-term implications of the investment and ensuring that the terms of the investment align with your company's overall goals. It's important to avoid making short-sighted decisions that may have negative consequences down the road.

V. Balancing the needs of investors with the needs of the business

Investors provide the necessary funds to fuel business growth, but in exchange, they often require some control or ownership stake in the company. To maintain a healthy relationship with investors while still ensuring the success of the business, it is essential to strike a balance between the two.

Here are some ways to balance the needs of investors and the needs of the business:

1. Clearly Define the Terms of the Investment: Before taking on any investment, it is crucial to clearly define the terms of the investment. This includes how much control investors will have over the company, what percentage of the company they will own, and what returns they can expect. By establishing clear terms from the beginning, both parties will have a better understanding of what to expect, reducing the potential for conflict down the line.

2. Establish communication and reporting standards: Maintaining good communication with investors is crucial for building trust and keeping them informed about the company's progress. Set up regular communication channels and reporting standards to provide investors with updates on business performance, milestones, and challenges. This will help ensure that investors remain engaged and supportive, even during difficult times.

3. Focus on long-term goals: Balancing the needs of investors with the needs of the business requires a long-term perspective. While investors may want to see quick returns on their investment, it is important to stay focused on the long-term goals of the business. This means making decisions that prioritise the company's growth and profitability over short-term gains.

4. Maintain a Strong Leadership Team: To build investor confidence, it is essential to have a strong leadership team in place that is capable of executing the business plan effectively. This includes having a clear vision for the company, a solid strategy for growth, and a team with the skills and expertise to execute on that plan.

5. Be Transparent and Honest: Honesty and transparency are keys to maintaining trust with investors. Be open and honest about the company's financial performance, challenges, and opportunities. If there are issues that may impact the business, communicate them as soon as possible to ensure that investors are fully informed.

6. Consider Alternative Funding Sources: Raising capital from investors is not the only way to fund a business. Consider alternative funding sources, such as loans or crowdfunding, that may allow you to maintain more control over your business while still accessing the necessary capital.

VI. Exit Strategies

An exit strategy refers to a plan for how an investor can eventually sell or divest their ownership stake in a company and realise a return on their investment. Exit strategies are important to consider when making an investment, as they can have a significant impact on the investor's returns and overall investment strategy. Here are some potential exit strategies for investors:

1. Selling the business: One of the most common exit strategies for investors is to sell their ownership stake in the company to a buyer. This can be done either through a private sale to another investor or through a strategic acquisition by another company. In either case, the investor will need to carefully consider the potential buyers and the valuation of the company in order to negotiate the best possible sale price.

2. Going Public: Another option for exit is to take the company public through an initial public offering (IPO). This involves selling shares of the company to the public, which can provide a significant return for early investors. However, going public can also be a complex and expensive process that requires significant preparation and planning.

3.Management Buyout: In some cases, the management team of the company may be interested in buying out the ownership stake of investors. This can be a good option for investors who want to sell their stake to a group of people who are intimately familiar with the business and its operations.

4. Liquidation: If none of the above options are viable, investors may need to consider a liquidation strategy. This involves selling off the company's assets and distributing the proceeds to investors. While this is generally not the most desirable outcome for investors, it may be necessary in certain situations.

When planning an exit strategy, investors need to consider a number of factors, including the potential valuation of the company, the potential buyers or investors, and the overall market conditions. It's also important to have a clear understanding of the company's finances and operations, as well as any potential legal or regulatory issues that may impact the exit strategy.

Ultimately, the success of an exit strategy will depend on a number of factors, including the timing of the sale, the negotiation of the sale price, and the market conditions at the time of the sale. By carefully considering all of these factors and planning ahead, investors can increase their chances of a successful exit and a profitable return on their investment.

VII. Conclusion

Raising funds and securing financing can be critical parts of growing a business, but they can also be a complex and challenging process. To succeed, it's important to understand the various financing options available and to carefully plan and prepare for each stage of the fundraising process.

Firstly, it's crucial to have a clear and well-defined business plan that clearly articulates your goals, target market, and competitive advantage. Having a compelling pitch and presentation materials can also help to communicate your vision and attract potential investors.

It's also important to consider a range of financing options, such as equity financing, debt financing, and government grants. Each option has its own pros and cons, so it's essential to carefully evaluate each one and choose the one that best fits your business needs.

In addition, it's important to avoid common fundraising pitfalls such as overestimating your valuation or underestimating the amount of capital you will need. It's also critical to maintain open and transparent communication with your investors and to keep them informed about your progress and any potential challenges you may be facing.

CHAPTER FIVE

Marketing and Sales

I. Introduction

Marketing and sales are two integral components of any successful business. Marketing is the process of identifying and satisfying customers' needs and wants through the creation, promotion, and distribution of goods and services. On the other hand, sales involve the process of converting interested prospects into paying customers by communicating the value of the products or services.

In today's highly competitive business environment, marketing and sales play a critical role in creating a sustainable business model. The ability to market and sell effectively is essential for any company looking to grow and succeed. A well-executed marketing and sales strategy can help businesses differentiate themselves from competitors, reach a larger audience, and generate more revenue.

The world of marketing and sales has undergone significant changes over the past few decades, primarily due to advancements in technology and the rise of social media. As a result, businesses now have access to a range of tools and platforms to reach customers in new and innovative ways. However, the fundamentals of marketing and sales remain the same, and it is essential for businesses to understand the core principles of these practices to be successful.

In this chapter, we will explore the basics of marketing and sales and examine how businesses can leverage these practices to achieve their objectives. We will also examine the latest trends and technologies in marketing and sales and discuss how businesses can use these tools to create effective strategies. By the end of this chapter, you should have a solid understanding of the principles and best practices of marketing and sales and be equipped with the knowledge to apply them to your business.

Importance of Marketing and Sales

Marketing and sales play a key role in attracting and retaining customers. Marketing is the process of identifying customers' needs and wants and creating products or services that fulfil those needs. Sales, on the other hand, involves convincing potential customers that the products or services are the best solution to meet their needs. Through effective marketing and sales strategies, businesses can attract and retain customers, leading to increased revenue and profitability.

Moreover, marketing and sales efforts can help businesses build brand awareness, which is essential for creating a sustainable business model. A strong brand can differentiate a business from its competitors, help it connect with customers, and build trust and loyalty. Effective marketing and sales strategies can help businesses establish a unique brand identity and create a strong brand image in the minds of their target audience.

In today's highly competitive business environment, marketing and sales are even more critical. With the rise of social media and other digital marketing channels, businesses have access to a range of tools and platforms to reach customers in new and innovative ways. However, the fundamentals of marketing and sales remain the same. To succeed, businesses must understand the core principles of these practices and be able to adapt to changing market conditions.

II. Marketing

Marketing is the process of identifying, anticipating, and satisfying customer needs and wants through the creation, promotion, and distribution of products or services. It is a critical business function that involves researching, planning, executing, and evaluating the effectiveness of strategies to attract and retain customers.

4 P's of Marketing:

The marketing mix, also known as the "four Ps of marketing," is a framework that businesses use to develop their marketing strategies. The four Ps are product, price, promotion, and place.

1. Product: A "product" is any good, service, or idea that satisfies the needs and wants of the target market. It can be tangible, such as a physical product like a car, or intangible, such as a service like insurance. The product includes its features, quality, design, packaging, branding, and any warranties or guarantees. To develop a successful product, businesses must identify the needs and wants of their target market and design a product that meets those needs in a unique and compelling way. They must also continuously improve and update their product to stay competitive in the market.

2. Price: The price refers to the amount of money customers pay for the product or service. It is a critical factor that influences the perceived value of the product and can determine the profitability of the business. The price of the product should be set based on a number of factors, such as production costs, competitor pricing, target market, and overall business strategy. Businesses must also consider the perceived value of the product and determine whether the price is affordable and attractive to the target market.

3. Promotion: Promotion refers to the activities that businesses undertake to communicate the value of their product to the target market. This can include advertising, personal selling, sales promotions, public relations, and direct marketing. The goal of promotion is to increase awareness of the product, generate interest, and ultimately drive sales. To develop an effective promotional strategy, businesses must consider the target market, the message they want to communicate, and the most effective channels to reach that market.

4. Place: Place refers to the distribution channels that businesses use to make their products available to customers. This can include physical locations such as stores, as well as online marketplaces, mobile applications, and other digital channels. The distribution channels used should be convenient for the target market and ensure that the product is readily available when and where the customer wants it. Businesses must consider factors such as transportation costs, inventory management, and customer preferences when selecting their distribution channels.

Market Search

Market research is the process of gathering and analysing information about a particular market, its customers, and its competition. It is a critical tool for businesses that want to make informed decisions about their marketing strategies, product development, and overall business operations. The goal of market research is to provide businesses with actionable insights that can help them understand the needs and preferences of their target market, identify new opportunities for growth, and develop effective marketing strategies.

Market research can be conducted through both primary and secondary research methods. Primary research involves collecting data directly from the source, such as through surveys, focus groups, or observation. Secondary research involves collecting data from existing sources, such as market reports, industry publications, and online databases.

The following are some of the key steps involved in conducting effective market research:

1. Defining the research objective: The first step in market research is to clearly define the research objective. This involves identifying the information that is needed and the purpose of the research.

2. Designing the research methodology: The next step is to design the research methodology that will be used to collect and analyse the data. This includes deciding on the research approach (qualitative or quantitative), selecting the research method (such as surveys, focus groups, or interviews), and developing the research instrument (such as a questionnaire or interview guide).

3. Collecting data: The next step is to collect data using the research methodology that was designed. This may involve conducting surveys, focus groups, or interviews, or using observation or other methods to gather data.

4. Analyzing the data: Once the data has been collected, it needs to be analysed to identify patterns, trends, and insights. This may involve using statistical analysis or other methods to identify relationships between variables and make sense of the data.

5. Reporting the findings: The final step in market research is to report the findings to the relevant stakeholders. This may involve preparing a report or presentation that summarises the key findings and recommendations.

Overall, market research is a critical tool for businesses that want to make informed decisions about their marketing strategies, product development, and overall business operations. By gathering and analysing data about their target market, customers, and competition, businesses can gain insights that can help them make more effective decisions and achieve their marketing objectives.

Target market segmentation

Target market segmentation is the process of dividing a larger market into smaller subgroups of customers who have similar needs, characteristics, or behaviours. This process allows businesses to focus their marketing efforts and resources on specific groups of customers who are more likely to be interested in their products or services.

There are several different ways to segment a target market, such as demographic, psychographic, geographic, and behavioural segmentation.

Demographic segmentation involves dividing a market into smaller groups based on demographic characteristics such as age, gender, income, education, and occupation. Psychographic segmentation divides a market based on the lifestyle, personality, values, and attitudes of customers. Geographic segmentation involves dividing a market based on location, such as country, region, city, or even neighbourhood. Behavioural segmentation divides a market based on the behaviour and actions of customers, such as their purchasing habits, usage patterns, and brand loyalty.

Once a business has identified its target market segments, it can create marketing strategies that are tailored to each segment's unique needs and preferences. This approach can increase the effectiveness of marketing campaigns, improve customer engagement, and ultimately drive sales and revenue for the business.

Branding and positioning

Branding and positioning are two essential components of marketing that help companies distinguish themselves from their competitors and communicate their value to their target audience. Here's a brief explanation of both concepts:

Branding:
Branding is the process of creating a unique identity for a company or product. This identity includes everything from the name, logo, colour scheme, and messaging to the company's mission, values, and personality. A strong brand helps to build trust, loyalty, and recognition among consumers, which can lead to increased sales and revenue. To build a strong brand, companies must consistently

deliver high-quality products or services, communicate their values effectively, and differentiate themselves from their competitors.

Positioning:

Positioning refers to the way a company or product is perceived by its target audience in relation to its competitors. It involves identifying the unique attributes of the product or service that differentiate it from the competition and communicating those attributes to the target audience. A strong positioning strategy helps to create a distinct image in the minds of consumers and can lead to increased sales and market share. Effective positioning can be achieved by conducting market research to understand customer needs, identifying the key benefits of the product or service, and communicating those benefits in a clear and compelling way.

Together, branding and positioning form the foundation of a company's marketing strategy and play a crucial role in creating a strong, recognisable brand that resonates with its target audience.

Marketing Channels

Marketing channels refer to the various ways in which businesses can reach and communicate with their target audience to promote their products or services. Marketing channels can be broadly classified into two types: online and offline.

Online Marketing Channels:

1. Social media marketing: This involves promoting a business or product on social media platforms such as Facebook, Instagram, Twitter, and LinkedIn.

2. Search Engine Marketing: This includes using paid ads, search engine optimization (SEO), and other strategies to rank higher on search engine results pages.

3. Email marketing: This involves using email to communicate with potential and existing customers.

4. Content marketing: This includes creating and publishing valuable content such as blogs, videos, and infographics to attract and engage customers.

5. Affiliate marketing: This involves partnering with other businesses or influencers to promote a product or service.

6. Display Advertising: This includes using banner ads and other visual ads to reach customers on websites and social media platforms.

Offline Marketing Channels:

1. Print Advertising: This includes using print media such as newspapers, magazines, and billboards to reach customers.

2. Direct mail marketing: This involves sending physical promotional materials such as flyers, brochures, and coupons directly to customers.

3. Telemarketing: This includes using phone calls to communicate with potential and existing customers.

4. Events and Sponsorships: This includes sponsoring or hosting events such as trade shows and sports events to promote a business or product.

5. Public Relations: This involves building relationships with the media and using press releases and other tactics to generate positive coverage for a business or product.

6. Word-of-Mouth Marketing: This includes leveraging satisfied customers to promote a business through referrals and recommendations to their friends and family.

III. Sales

Sales in business refers to the process of generating revenue by selling products or services to customers. Sales activities may include prospecting for potential customers, building relationships with existing customers, identifying their needs and preferences, presenting product or service options, negotiating pricing and contracts, closing deals, and providing after-sales support. The ultimate goal of sales is to generate revenue and increase the profitability of a business.

Sales strategy and planning

Sales strategy refers to the overall approach and plan that a business uses to achieve its sales objectives. A sales strategy may include setting sales targets, identifying target customers and market segments, developing sales channels and processes, establishing pricing and discount policies, creating sales collateral and marketing materials, and defining sales metrics and performance indicators. The sales strategy should be aligned with the overall business strategy and take into account market trends, competitive dynamics, and customer preferences.

Sales planning is the process of developing a detailed plan of action to execute the sales strategy. It involves identifying specific actions, timelines, and responsibilities to achieve the sales goals set by the business. Sales planning may include setting up sales territories and quotas, establishing sales processes and systems, training sales staff, creating promotional and advertising campaigns, and developing lead generation and nurturing programs. Sales planning should be a continuous process, regularly reviewed and updated to reflect changes in the market and the business environment.

Sales Process

The sales process is a structured approach that guides the steps that a salesperson takes to successfully sell a product or service. There are different versions of the sales process, but one of the most commonly used is the following five-step process:

1. **Prospecting:** Prospecting is the first step in the sales process, which involves identifying potential customers or leads who might be interested in purchasing the product or service. Salespeople can use a variety of methods for prospecting, including online research, referrals from existing customers, trade shows, cold calling, and direct mail campaigns. The goal of this stage is to create a list of potential customers and determine which ones are worth pursuing.

2. **Qualifying:** Once a list of potential customers is created, the next step is to determine whether they are a good fit for the product or service being offered. This stage is called qualifying, and it involves researching the potential customer's needs, budget, decision-making process, and timeframe. The goal of this stage is to prioritise the leads and focus on the ones that are most likely to result in a sale.

3. **Presenting:** After qualifying the leads, the salesperson will move on to the presentation stage, which involves demonstrating the product or service and showing how it can solve the potential customer's needs. In this stage, the salesperson will use a variety of tools and techniques, including presentations, demos, and product samples. The goal of this stage is to build rapport with the

potential customer and convince them that the product or service is the best solution for their needs.

4. Handling Objections: Even after a successful presentation, potential customers may still have concerns or objections about the product or service. This stage involves addressing those objections and providing additional information or reassurance to overcome any doubts or hesitations. The goal of this stage is to build trust with the potential customer and address any concerns that might be preventing them from making a purchase.

5. Closing: The final stage of the sales process is closing, which involves asking the potential customer to make a purchase. This stage can involve a variety of closing techniques, including the assumptive close, the summary close, or the urgency close. The goal of this stage is to secure the sale and create a satisfied customer who may become a repeat customer and provide referrals.

Sales Management and Training

Sales management is the process of leading and directing a sales team to achieve the company's sales goals. Effective sales management involves developing strategies, setting targets, managing resources, and motivating and coaching the sales team to perform at their best. The main functions of sales management include:

1. Sales planning: Developing a sales plan that aligns with the overall business strategy, setting sales targets, and defining sales territories

2. Sales organization: Establishing the sales structure, designing roles and responsibilities, and assigning tasks and resources to team members

3.Sales operations: Managing day-to-day sales activities, including prospecting, lead generation, customer acquisition, and order processing.

4. Sales analysis: Collecting and analysing sales data to track performance, identify trends, and make data-driven decisions to improve sales results.

5.Sales coaching and development: Providing training and coaching to sales reps to improve their skills, knowledge, and performance and helping them achieve their personal and professional goals.

Sales training is the process of educating and developing salespeople to become more effective in their roles. Effective sales training should be ongoing and cover a range of topics, including product knowledge, sales techniques, objection handling, customer relationship management, and negotiation skills. Some key steps in designing a sales training programme include:

1. Assessing needs: Identifying the skills and knowledge gaps in the sales team and determining what training is needed to address them.

2. Developing content: Creating training materials, including presentations, videos, role-playing exercises, and online courses, to support the training objectives

3. Delivering training: Choosing the right delivery method for the training, such as in-person training, virtual training, or self-paced learning

4. Measuring effectiveness: Evaluating the effectiveness of the training by measuring changes in behaviour, knowledge, and skills and monitoring the impact on sales results

Key Performance Indicators (KPIs)

Key performance indicators (KPIs) are a set of measurable metrics used to evaluate and track the performance of a business or specific areas of a business. In sales, KPIs are used to track and measure the success of a sales team or an individual sales representative.

Here are some common KPIs used in sales:

1.Sales Revenue: This is the total amount of revenue generated from sales. It is an essential KPI as it directly indicates the financial success of the sales team.

2. Sales Growth: This KPI measures the percentage increase or decrease in sales over a specified period. A high growth rate is a good indication of a successful sales team.

3. Conversion Rate: This KPI measures the percentage of leads that convert into sales. A high conversion rate indicates the sales team is efficient at closing deals.

4.Average Deal Size: This KPI measures the average amount of revenue generated per sale. It is a good indicator of the effectiveness of the sales team at selling high-value products or services.

5.Sales Cycle Length: This KPI measures the average time it takes to close a deal from the initial lead. A shorter sales cycle is a good indication of an efficient sales team.

6. Customer Acquisition Cost (CAC): This KPI measures the cost of acquiring a new customer. It is an essential metric to track, as a high CAC can negatively impact profitability.

7. Customer Lifetime Value (CLV): This KPI measures the total revenue a customer is expected to generate over their lifetime. It is an essential metric as it helps to prioritise customer acquisition and retention efforts.

8. Sales Pipeline: This KPI measures the number of potential deals in the sales pipeline. It is an essential metric as it helps predict future sales revenue.

9. Sales Activities: This KPI measures the number of sales-related activities performed by a salesperson. These activities could include calls, emails, and meetings.

By tracking these KPIs, sales managers can monitor the performance of the sales team and take necessary actions to improve it.

IV. *Marketing and Sales Alignment*

Marketing and sales alignment refers to the process of coordinating and integrating the efforts of a company's marketing and sales teams towards common goals and objectives. The goal of alignment is to create a seamless, coordinated approach to lead generation, prospect nurturing, and customer acquisition that ultimately leads to revenue growth.

Marketing and sales alignment involves establishing shared goals and metrics, developing a common understanding of the target audience and their needs, and creating an integrated approach to lead generation, lead scoring, and lead qualification. The alignment also involves improving communication and collaboration between the two teams, as well as sharing information and feedback on marketing campaigns and sales performance.

When marketing and sales teams are aligned, they can work together more effectively to create a consistent and compelling customer experience. Marketing can provide sales with better leads, insights on target customers, and content that supports the sales process. Sales can provide marketing with feedback on the effectiveness of their campaigns, the quality of the leads, and the customer journey, which can help refine and improve marketing strategies.

The Importance of Alignment

Alignment is crucial for any organisation to achieve its goals and objectives. It refers to the coordination and integration of different parts of the organisation towards common goals, objectives, and strategies.

One of the main benefits of alignment is better coordination. When different departments and teams within an organisation are working in harmony towards common objectives, it leads to better communication, collaboration, and coordination among teams. This reduces duplication of efforts and increases efficiency, which ultimately leads to better outcomes.

Alignment also improves productivity. When different parts of an organisation are aligned, it leads to better productivity. Teams can work together more effectively, reducing delays and mistakes in the process. This results in faster project completion and better use of resources.

Another benefit of alignment is increased employee engagement. When employees understand how their work fits into the larger goals and objectives of the organization, they are more likely to be motivated and engaged in their work. This can lead to higher job satisfaction, lower turnover rates, and improved performance.

Alignment also helps to create a consistent customer experience. When different parts of the organisation are aligned, it leads to a consistent approach to customer interactions. This improves customer satisfaction and loyalty and ultimately helps drive revenue growth.

Tools and Techniques for Alignment

There are various tools and techniques that organisations can use to achieve alignment between different parts of the organization, such as lead generation, lead nurturing, and sales enablement. Here are some examples:

1. Lead generation: This involves creating awareness and interest in a product or service and identifying potential customers who are likely to be interested in what the organisation is offering. Lead generation can be done through a variety of channels, such as email marketing, social media, content marketing, and search engine optimization (SEO). By generating leads, both the marketing and sales teams have a pool of potential customers to work with.

2. Lead nurturing: Once leads have been generated, it is important to nurture them through the sales funnel by providing them with relevant information and building a relationship with them. Lead nurturing can be done through email marketing, social media, and other personalised communication channels. By nurturing leads, the marketing and sales teams can build trust with potential customers and increase the likelihood of converting them into paying customers.

3. Sales enablement: Sales enablement refers to the tools, processes, and resources that are provided to the sales team to help them sell more effectively. This can include sales training, sales collateral, and sales automation tools. By providing the sales team with the right tools and resources, they can sell more effectively and close more deals.

4. Customer relationship management (CRM): A CRM system can be used to manage customer interactions and data throughout the customer lifecycle. By using a CRM system, both the marketing and sales teams can have access to the same data about customers and their interactions with the organization. This can help both teams work together more effectively and provide a better customer experience.

By using these tools and techniques, organisations can align their marketing and sales teams and work towards a common goal of generating revenue. This alignment can help improve the efficiency and effectiveness of both teams, ultimately leading to increased revenue for the organization.

V. Market and Sales Analytics

Marketing and sales analytics are techniques and tools used to analyse customer data and behaviour to optimise marketing and sales strategies. Marketing analytics involves collecting and analysing data from various marketing channels, such as social media, email, and search engines, to evaluate the effectiveness of marketing campaigns. It helps businesses understand customer behaviour, preferences, and how they interact with various marketing channels. By using marketing analytics, businesses can optimise their marketing strategies to increase customer engagement, conversion rates, and revenue.

Sales analytics involves analysing sales data to identify trends, patterns, and customer behaviour. It helps businesses understand their sales pipeline and predict future sales. Sales analytics can provide insights on the most profitable products or services, customer buying patterns, and the performance of the sales team. By analysing sales data, businesses can optimise their sales strategies to increase revenue and customer satisfaction.

Marketing and sales analytics can provide businesses with valuable insights to improve the customer experience, increase customer engagement, and drive revenue growth. They are essential tools for businesses looking to make data-driven decisions and stay ahead of the competition.

Importance of Analytics

Analytics refers to the systematic analysis of data or statistics to extract insights, patterns, and trends that can help organisations make data-driven decisions. The importance of analytics can be summed up in the following points:

1. Better decision-making: Analytics helps businesses make data-driven decisions. By analysing data, businesses can identify patterns, trends, and anomalies that would otherwise remain hidden. This allows them to make informed decisions, anticipate changes, and respond quickly to market shifts.

2. Improved efficiency: By analysing data, organisations can identify inefficiencies in their processes and operations. This helps them to streamline their workflows, eliminate waste, and optimise their resources, which leads to increased efficiency and cost savings.

3. Enhanced customer experience: Analytics can help businesses better understand their customers' needs, preferences, and behaviours. This allows them to create personalised and targeted marketing campaigns, improve their products and services, and provide a better customer experience.

4. Competitive advantage: Analytics provides insights that can help businesses gain a competitive advantage over their rivals. By understanding market trends and consumer behaviour, organisations can stay ahead of their competitors and make better strategic decisions.

5. Improved risk management: Analytics can help businesses identify potential risks and threats and develop proactive strategies to manage them. By analysing data and identifying patterns, businesses can anticipate and respond to potential risks before they become major issues.

Key Marketing and Sales Metrics

There are numerous marketing and sales metrics that businesses can track to evaluate the effectiveness of their marketing and sales efforts. Here are some of the key metrics:

1. Customer Acquisition Cost (CAC): CAC is the total cost of acquiring a new customer, including marketing and sales expenses. It is important to track CAC to ensure that the cost of acquiring a customer does not exceed the revenue generated from that customer.

2. Conversion Rate: The conversion rate is the percentage of visitors who take a desired action on a website, such as making a purchase, filling out a form, or subscribing to a newsletter. A high conversion rate indicates that the website is effectively engaging visitors and converting them into customers.

3. Customer Lifetime Value (CLV): CLV is the amount of revenue that a customer generates over the course of their relationship with a business. CLV is an important metric to track because it helps businesses understand the value of each customer and make informed decisions about marketing and sales strategies.

4.Sales Growth: Sales growth is the rate at which a business's sales are increasing over a period of time.

Tracking sales growth can help businesses identify areas for improvement and evaluate the effectiveness of their marketing and sales strategies.

5. Return on Investment (ROI): ROI is the ratio of the revenue generated by a marketing or sales campaign to the cost of the campaign. ROI is an important metric to track because it helps businesses evaluate the profitability of their marketing and sales efforts.

6.Customer Churn Rate: The churn rate is the percentage of customers who stop using a business's product or service over a period of time. Tracking churn rate can help businesses identify areas for improvement in their product or service and retention strategies.

By tracking these key marketing and sales metrics, businesses can make data-driven decisions and optimise their marketing and sales strategies to increase revenue and customer satisfaction.

Tools and techniques for measuring marketing and sales effectiveness

There are various tools and techniques available for measuring marketing and sales effectiveness. Here are some of the commonly used ones:

1. Customer surveys are a great tool for collecting feedback from customers about their experiences with a business. This can help businesses identify areas for improvement in their marketing and sales strategies.

2. Web analytics: Tools like Google Analytics can provide businesses with insights into their website traffic, user behaviour, and conversion rates. These tools can help businesses optimise their websites and improve their marketing and sales strategies.

3.Sales Reporting: Sales reporting tools can help businesses track their sales performance over time and identify trends and patterns. This can help businesses make informed decisions about their sales strategies.

4. Social Media Monitoring: Social media monitoring tools can help businesses track and analyse their social media activity. This can help businesses identify customer sentiment, engagement levels, and opportunities for improvement.

5. Email Analytics: Email analytics tools can help businesses track email campaign performance, including open rates, click-through rates, and conversion rates. This can help businesses optimise their email marketing strategies.

6. A/B Testing: A/B testing is a technique that involves testing two different versions of a marketing or sales campaign to see which performs better. This can help businesses optimise their campaigns for maximum effectiveness.

VI. Case Study and Example

Nike's "Just Do It" Campaign

Nike's "Just Do It" campaign is a great example of successful marketing. The campaign was launched in 1988 and has since become one of the most recognisable and successful slogans in the world. The campaign was designed to inspire athletes to push themselves to their limits and achieve their goals, and it has been a huge success. Nike's marketing team worked hard to create a slogan and brand that were simple, memorable, and impactful. This is an excellent example of how effective marketing can help a brand become a household name.

Apple's iPhone launch

The launch of Apple's iPhone in 2007 is another great example of successful marketing and sales. The iPhone was a game-changing product that revolutionised the way we communicate and interact with technology. Apple's marketing team built up hype for the product with a series of teaser ads and public demonstrations, and the launch was a huge success. Apple sold 1.39 million iPhones in the first year, and the product went on to become one of the most successful consumer electronics products in history. This is an excellent example of how effective marketing and sales can help a new product take off and become a huge success.

Coca-Cola's "Share a Coke" Campaign

Coca-Cola's "Share a Coke" campaign is another great example of successful marketing. The campaign was launched in 2011 and was designed to encourage people to share their Coca-Cola with friends and family. Coca-Cola replaced their traditional branding with common first names and nicknames, so consumers could find bottles with their own name or the names of their loved ones. The campaign was a huge success, with sales increasing by 2.5% in the first month alone. This is an excellent example of how effective marketing can help create an emotional connection with consumers and increase sales.

Amazon's Personalized Recommendations

Amazon's personalised recommendation system is a great example of successful sales. Amazon's algorithm analyses the buying patterns of each customer and suggests products that are likely to be of interest to them. This system has been incredibly effective at increasing sales, with some estimates suggesting that personalised recommendations account for up to 35% of Amazon's total revenue. This is an excellent example of how effective sales can help to increase revenue by providing customers with products that they are likely to be interested in.

Zara's Fast Fashion Model

Zara's fast-fashion model is another great example of successful marketing and sales. Zara is able to quickly identify and respond to emerging fashion trends by using data analytics and a highly efficient supply chain. This allows them to bring new products to market much faster than their competitors, which has helped them become one of the most successful fashion brands in the world. This is an excellent example of how effective marketing and sales can help a brand differentiate themselves from their competitors and become a market leader.

Key Points to Remember

1. Know Your Target Audience: One of the most important lessons in marketing and sales is to know your target audience. Understanding your customers' needs, preferences, and behaviours is essential to developing effective marketing campaigns and driving sales.

2. Develop a Strong Brand Identity: A strong brand identity is crucial to building customer loyalty and trust. By creating a unique and memorable brand, companies can differentiate themselves from competitors and build a strong customer base.

3. Utilize Data Analytics: Data analytics can provide valuable insights into customer behaviour and preferences. By analysing data from sales, customer interactions, and other sources, companies can make informed decisions about their marketing and sales strategies.

4. Experiment and iterate: Marketing and sales are constantly evolving, and what works today may not work tomorrow. Companies should be willing to experiment with new strategies and adapt their approach as needed.

5. Provide Excellent Customer Service: Providing excellent customer service is key to building a strong and loyal customer base. Companies should focus on providing timely and responsive support, addressing customer concerns and complaints, and going above and beyond to exceed customer expectations.

6. Focus on Customer Retention: While acquiring new customers is important, retaining existing customers is equally crucial. Companies should focus on building long-term relationships with their customers by providing personalised experiences and incentives for repeat business.

7. Align Sales and Marketing: Sales and marketing teams should work closely together to ensure a consistent message and approach. By aligning their efforts, companies can create a more cohesive and effective marketing and sales strategy.

8.Embrace Digital Marketing: Digital marketing channels, such as social media, email marketing, and search engine optimization, are essential to reaching modern customers. Companies should invest in digital marketing and continually adapt their strategies to keep up with the latest trends and technologies.

VII. Future Trends and Opportunities

There are many emerging marketing and sales technologies that businesses can use to improve their operations and grow their customer base. Here are some examples:

1. Artificial Intelligence (AI): AI is increasingly being used in marketing and sales to help businesses analyse customer data, create personalised marketing campaigns, and make better decisions. For example, chatbots can use AI to provide customer service support 24/7, while AI-powered tools can analyse customer data to provide insights into customer behaviour and preferences.

2. Machine learning: Machine learning is a subset of AI that involves algorithms that can learn from data and improve over time. In marketing and sales, machine learning can be used to predict customer behaviour, identify patterns, and optimise marketing campaigns. For example, a machine learning algorithm can analyse customer data to determine which products are likely to be most popular and adjust marketing campaigns accordingly.

3. Augmented reality (AR): AR technology is increasingly being used in marketing and sales to provide customers with an immersive and interactive experience. For example, retailers can use AR to create virtual try-on experiences for clothing and beauty products, while real estate companies can use AR to provide virtual tours of properties.

4. Internet of Things (IoT): IoT refers to a network of connected devices that can communicate with each other and share data. In marketing and sales, IoT can be used to gather data on customer behaviour and preferences. For example, a smart fridge can track a customer's food preferences and suggest new products based on that data.

5. Blockchain: Blockchain is a decentralised ledger technology that can be used to securely store and share data. In marketing and sales, blockchain can be used to improve supply chain transparency and reduce fraud. For example, a blockchain-based platform can be used to track the origin of products and ensure that they are ethically sourced.

6. Virtual reality (VR): VR is a technology that provides a fully immersive experience for users. In marketing and sales, VR can be used to create interactive and engaging experiences for customers. For example, car companies can use VR to provide virtual test drives for potential customers.

7. Big Data Analytics: Big Data analytics involves the use of large amounts of data to identify patterns and insights. In marketing and sales, big data analytics can be used to understand customer behaviour, predict trends, and optimise marketing campaigns.

8. Predictive Analytics: Predictive analytics is a subset of big data analytics that involves the use of statistical algorithms to make predictions about future events. In marketing and sales, predictive analytics can be used to forecast sales trends, identify new customers, and optimise pricing.

9. Customer Relationship Management (CRM) Software: CRM software is a tool that businesses can use to manage customer interactions and data. In marketing and sales, CRM software can be used to track customer behaviour, analyse data, and improve customer retention.

10. Social Listening Tools: Social listening tools are software applications that can be used to monitor social media channels for mentions of a brand, product, or service. In marketing and sales, social listening tools can be used to gather customer feedback, identify trends, and adjust marketing campaigns.

Changes in Customer Behaviour and Expectations

Customer behaviour and expectations are constantly evolving, and businesses need to keep up with these changes in order to remain competitive. Here are some key changes in customer behaviour and expectations:

1. Increased Demand for Convenience: Customers today are looking for convenient ways to shop and access products and services. This has led to the rise of online shopping, mobile apps, and other digital channels that allow customers to make purchases from anywhere at any time.

2. Personalization: Customers expect businesses to provide personalised experiences that are tailored to their individual needs and preferences. This includes personalised product recommendations, targeted marketing campaigns, and customised customer service interactions.

3. Emphasis on Sustainability: Customers are increasingly concerned about environmental issues and are looking for businesses that are committed to sustainability. This includes offering eco-friendly products, reducing waste, and using sustainable business practices.

4. Greater Transparency: Customers today expect businesses to be transparent about their operations and practices. This includes providing clear information about product ingredients, sourcing, and ethical practices, as well as being open and honest about any issues that may arise.

5. Focus on Experience: Customers are looking for experiences that go beyond just buying a product or service. This includes providing excellent customer service, creating immersive and engaging retail environments, and offering unique and memorable experiences.

6. Demand for Speed: Customers expect fast and efficient service, whether it's in-store or online. This includes quick and easy checkout processes, fast shipping times, and responsive customer service.

7. Mobile First: With the increasing use of smartphones, customers are looking for mobile-optimized experiences that are easy to use and navigate. This includes mobile-optimized websites, mobile apps, and mobile-friendly customer service interactions.

Overall, businesses that can understand and adapt to these changes in customer behaviour and expectations are more likely to succeed in today's marketplace. By providing convenient, personalized, and sustainable experiences, businesses can build strong relationships with customers and gain a competitive advantage.

Opportunities and growth

There are many opportunities for innovation and growth in today's marketplace. Here are some examples:

1.Digital Transformation: As more and more customers shift their buying habits online, businesses have an opportunity to invest in digital transformation and create new and innovative online experiences. This can include creating mobile apps, developing e-commerce websites, and leveraging digital marketing strategies to reach new customers.

2. Personalization: Personalization is an important trend in customer behaviour and expectations, and businesses that can provide personalised experiences are likely to succeed. This can include using customer data to create targeted marketing campaigns, offering personalised product recommendations, and providing customised customer service interactions.

3. Sustainability: Businesses that can demonstrate their commitment to sustainability have an opportunity to differentiate themselves from their competitors and attract environmentally conscious customers. This can include using eco-friendly materials, reducing waste, and implementing sustainable business practices.

4. Artificial Intelligence (AI): AI is an emerging technology that offers many opportunities for innovation and growth in marketing and sales. Businesses can use AI to analyse customer data, make better decisions, and create personalised experiences.

5. Mobile-first: With the increasing use of smartphones, businesses that can create mobile-optimized experiences are likely to succeed. This can include developing mobile apps, creating mobile-friendly websites, and providing mobile-friendly customer service interactions.

6. Customer Experience: Businesses that can create excellent customer experiences have the opportunity to build strong relationships with customers and gain a competitive advantage. This can include providing exceptional customer service, creating immersive and engaging retail environments, and offering unique and memorable experiences.

7. Data Analytics: Data analytics is a powerful tool that businesses can use to gather insights into customer behaviour and make better decisions. By leveraging data analytics, businesses can optimise their operations, identify new customers, and forecast sales trends.

VIII. *Conclusion*

Marketing and sales are critical components of any successful business. These two functions are interconnected and can determine the success of any business. The primary objective of marketing is to promote a product or service by creating a connection between the product or service and the customer. On the other hand, sales focus on the actual process of selling the product or service.

A company that has a well-defined and effective marketing and sales strategy is well-positioned to grow and expand. Developing a marketing and sales strategy involves understanding the target audience, crafting a value proposition that meets their needs, and developing a marketing mix that speaks directly to their interests. The marketing mix includes product, price, place, and promotion. Each of these elements is critical to the success of the marketing and sales plan.

In developing a marketing and sales plan, it is essential to take a holistic approach that encompasses all aspects of the customer journey, from the initial contact to the final sale. In the past, the focus was on selling products, but now the focus is on meeting the needs of the customer. This approach involves understanding the customer's pain points, what motivates them, and their buying behaviours. Armed with this knowledge, businesses can develop a marketing and sales strategy that speaks directly to their customers' needs.

One of the most critical factors in marketing and sales is the ability to measure performance. It is essential to have a system in place that tracks and measures the effectiveness of the marketing and sales plan. Key performance indicators (KPIs) such as website traffic, conversion rates, customer acquisition costs, and customer retention rates can help businesses determine how well their marketing and sales plan is working. By measuring these KPIs, businesses can identify areas that need improvement and make the necessary changes to optimise their marketing and sales strategies.

It is also critical for businesses to stay up-to-date with the latest technology and marketing and sales trends. There is an ever-increasing amount of data available, and it is essential to be able to use this data to gain insights into customer behaviour and preferences. Technology can be used to automate marketing and sales processes and provide a personalised customer experience. These trends can help businesses stay ahead of the competition and improve the overall effectiveness of their marketing and sales strategies.

Finally, businesses need to be aware of legal and ethical considerations in marketing and sales. It is important to ensure that all marketing and sales activities are in compliance with the law and adhere to ethical principles. Failure to do so can result in serious consequences, including loss of reputation, legal action, and financial penalties.

CHAPTER SIX

Managing Your Business

I. Introduction

Business management is the process of organising and coordinating the resources and activities of a business to achieve specific goals and objectives. It involves planning, directing, and controlling the operations of an organisation to ensure the efficient and effective use of resources.

Business management can include a wide range of activities, such as setting goals and objectives, developing strategies to achieve those goals, creating budgets, overseeing the production of goods and services, managing employees and human resources, and monitoring financial performance.

A business manager is responsible for overseeing the day-to-day operations of a business, making decisions about the allocation of resources, and ensuring that the business is operating efficiently and effectively. This requires a strong understanding of finance, marketing, operations, and human resources, as well as the ability to communicate effectively with employees, customers, and other stakeholders.

Effective business management is essential for the success of any organization. By establishing clear goals and objectives, creating a plan for achieving those goals, and ensuring that resources are used efficiently and effectively, a business can improve its performance, increase profitability, and create a strong foundation for future growth and success.

Importance of Effective Business

Effective business management is important for the success and sustainability of any organization, regardless of its size or industry. Here are some of the key reasons why effective business management is important:

1. **Achieving business objectives:** Effective management ensures that the business is run in a way that aligns with its goals and objectives. This involves setting clear targets, developing strategies to achieve them, and ensuring that everyone in the organisation is working towards the same objectives.

2. **Increased productivity:** Good management practices can improve productivity by streamlining processes, optimising resources, and improving communication and collaboration within the organization.

3. **Better decision-making:** Effective management involves making informed decisions based on accurate data and analysis. This helps to minimise risks and make more strategic and effective choices for the business.

4. **Improved employee morale:** When employees are managed effectively, they feel valued, supported, and motivated. This can lead to increased job satisfaction, higher levels of engagement, and lower staff turnover.

5. Enhanced customer satisfaction: Effective management helps to create a culture of customer service excellence, which in turn can improve customer satisfaction levels and lead to increased loyalty and repeat business.

6.Financial stability: Good management practices can help to ensure the financial stability of a business by managing costs, maximising revenue, and creating a robust financial plan for the future.

II. Establishing Your Business Management Framework

The business management framework provides a structured approach for managing the day-to-day operations of a business and achieving its long-term goals and objectives. In this article, we will discuss the key components of a business management framework, which include defining business goals and objectives, identifying key performance indicators (KPIs), and developing a strategic plan.

1. Defining Business Goals and Objectives:

The first step in establishing a business management framework is to define your business goals and objectives. Business goals are long-term outcomes that you want to achieve, such as increasing revenue, expanding into new markets, or improving customer satisfaction. Objectives, on the other hand, are specific, measurable, and time-bound targets that support the overall business goals. For example, if your goal is to increase revenue, your objectives may include increasing sales by a certain percentage, launching new products or services, or reducing costs.

Defining business goals and objectives requires careful consideration of your business's strengths, weaknesses, opportunities, and threats (SWOT analysis). You should also take into account your target market, industry trends, and competitive landscape. Once you have identified your goals and objectives, you can create a roadmap for achieving them.

2. Identifying Key Performance Indicators (KPIs):

Key performance indicators (KPIs) are measurable values that help you track progress towards your business goals and objectives. KPIs provide a quantifiable way to evaluate the success of your business and identify areas that require improvement. By tracking KPIs, you can make data-driven decisions and adjust your strategies as needed.

To identify the right KPIs for your business, you need to consider the specific goals and objectives you have set. For example, if your goal is to increase revenue, some KPIs you may track include sales growth, customer acquisition cost, customer lifetime value, and gross profit margin. If your objective is to improve customer satisfaction, you may track KPIs such as net promoter score (NPS), customer retention rate, or customer complaints resolved.

It's important to note that KPIs should be SMART: specific, measureable, achievable, relevant, and time-bound. This means that each KPI should have a clear definition, a quantifiable measure, and a specific timeline for achieving it. By setting SMART KPIs, you can ensure that you're tracking the right metrics and that your efforts are focused on achieving your business goals and objectives.

3. Developing a Strategic Plan:

A strategic plan is a roadmap that outlines how you will achieve your business goals and objectives. It includes a series of actionable steps that you will take to move your business forward. Developing a strategic plan requires you to consider all aspects of your business, including marketing, operations, finance, and human resources.

The first step in developing a strategic plan is to identify the critical success factors for your business. These are the key areas that you need to focus on to achieve your goals and objectives. For example, if your goal is to increase revenue, your critical success factors may include launching new products or services, improving your sales process, or expanding your market reach.

Once you have identified your critical success factors, you can create a set of actionable steps to achieve them. These steps should be specific, measurable, and time-bound, and they should be aligned with your KPIs. You should also assign responsibilities for each step and establish a timeline for completion.

In addition to creating a strategic plan, it's essential to monitor your progress regularly. This means tracking your KPIs, reviewing your strategies, and making adjustments as needed. By monitoring your progress, you can identify areas that are working well and those that require improvement. You can then adjust your strategies to achieve your goals and objectives.

What happens when you don't manage your business properly?

I want to share a short story of a person who managed his business poorly. This story shows how important it is to manage a business properly. Even a small mistake can have a significant impact on the success of the business.

Once upon a time, there was a man who had a small grocery store in his town. He started the business with a lot of passion and dedication, and soon his store became very popular among the locals. However, he had a tendency to be very careless when it came to managing his business.

He didn't keep track of his inventory, and as a result, many of his popular items were often out of stock. He was also very casual when it came to keeping the store clean, which made it unattractive to customers. He didn't pay attention to the competition and was charging high prices for his products compared to other stores in the area.

Initially, the loyal customers of the store didn't mind the small issues, but over time, these problems started to affect his sales. The customers began to complain about the lack of products and the high prices, and soon they started to shop elsewhere. Word of mouth spread, and the once-popular grocery store started to lose more and more customers.

He didn't take these issues seriously, and he continued to manage his business in the same careless way. He ignored the warning signs and didn't take any steps to improve his business. As a result, his sales continued to decline, and he started to accumulate debt.

Eventually, his store had to shut down due to lack of business, and he was forced to declare bankruptcy. The once-successful grocery store that he had built with so much passion and hard work is now gone.

This story shows how important it is to pay attention to customer feedback, keep track of inventory, and stay up-to-date with the competition to stay ahead in the market.

III. Financial Management

Financial management is the process of managing an organization's financial resources to achieve its goals and objectives. It involves planning, organizing, controlling, and monitoring financial activities to ensure that the organization's financial resources are used efficiently and effectively.

Budgeting and Forecasting

Budgeting and forecasting are key components of financial management that help organisations plan and allocate resources to meet their strategic goals and objectives.

Budgeting is the process of creating a financial plan for a specific period, typically a year, that details the expected income and expenses of the organization. It involves estimating revenue and expenses and setting financial goals and targets for the organization. A budget is an essential tool for monitoring the financial performance of an organisation and making informed financial decisions.

Forecasting, on the other hand, is the process of predicting future financial performance based on historical data and trends. It involves analysing past financial performance to identify patterns and trends and using that information to predict future financial outcomes. Forecasting can be used to estimate revenue and expenses, as well as to identify potential risks and opportunities for the organization.

Budgeting and forecasting are closely related, as budgeting is often based on forecasts of future financial performance. By combining budgeting and forecasting, organisations can create a more accurate financial plan that takes future trends, potential risks, and opportunities into account. This enables organisations to make informed financial decisions and allocate resources more effectively.

Financial Report and Analysis

Financial reporting and analysis are key components of financial management that involve the preparation and interpretation of financial information to support decision-making and monitor the financial performance of an organization.

Financial reporting involves the preparation of financial statements, such as the balance sheet, income statement, and statement of cash flows, that provide a summary of the organization's financial activities over a given period. Financial reporting is essential for stakeholders, such as investors, creditors, and regulators, to assess the financial health of the organisation and make informed decisions.

Financial analysis, on the other hand, involves the interpretation and evaluation of financial statements and other financial data to gain insights into the financial performance of the organization. Financial analysis can be used to identify trends and patterns in the organization's financial performance, as well as to compare the organization's financial performance to industry benchmarks and that of competitors.

Financial analysis techniques include ratio analysis, trend analysis, and variance analysis, which help identify areas of strength and weakness in the organization's financial performance. The insights gained from financial analysis can be used to make informed financial decisions and to develop strategies to improve the organization's financial performance.

Cash Flow Management

Cash flow management is an essential component of financial management that involves the management of the inflow and outflow of cash in a company. Cash flow is the amount of cash and cash equivalents that flow in and out of a business. Cash flow management involves managing the timing and amount of cash inflows and outflows to ensure that a company has enough cash to meet its financial obligations and take advantage of investment opportunities. In this article, we will discuss the importance of cash flow management, the tools and techniques used in cash flow management, and how to implement effective cash flow management in a business.

The importance of cash flow management

Firstly, managing cash flow helps businesses maintain liquidity. Liquidity is the ability of a business to meet its financial obligations as and when they fall due. A business that is short on cash may find it difficult to meet its obligations and may even become insolvent. Managing cash flow helps to ensure that a business has enough cash on hand to meet its financial obligations and to take advantage of investment opportunities.

Secondly, cash flow management helps businesses make informed financial decisions. By monitoring cash inflows and outflows, businesses can identify areas where they can reduce costs and increase revenue. For example, a business may identify that it is spending too much on marketing and advertising and decide to reduce these costs to improve profitability.

Thirdly, cash flow management helps businesses plan for the future. By monitoring cash inflows and outflows, businesses can project future cash flows and plan accordingly. This can help businesses avoid cash shortages and take advantage of investment opportunities as they arise.

Tools and Techniques Used in Cash Flow Management

There are several tools and techniques used in cash flow management. The most common include:

1. Cash Flow Statements: Cash flow statements are financial statements that show the inflows and outflows of cash in a business. These statements are typically prepared on a monthly basis and provide a detailed picture of a company's cash position. Cash flow statements can be used to identify trends and patterns in cash inflows and outflows, which can help businesses make informed financial decisions.

2. Accounts Receivable Management: Accounts receivable management involves managing the amounts owed to a business by its customers. This includes tracking invoices and payments, as well as following up on overdue payments. Effective accounts receivable management can help businesses maintain cash flow by ensuring that payments are received in a timely manner.

3. Accounts Payable Management: Accounts payable management involves managing the amounts owed by a business to its suppliers and creditors. This includes tracking invoices and payments, as well as negotiating payment terms. Effective accounts payable management can help businesses manage their cash flow by ensuring that payments are made on time and that payment terms are favourable.

4. Inventory Management: Inventory management involves managing the levels of inventory in a business. This includes tracking inventory levels, forecasting demand, and ordering inventory as needed. Effective inventory management can help businesses manage their cash flow by ensuring that they have enough inventory to meet demand without tying up too much cash in excess inventory.

5. Budgeting: Budgeting is the process of creating a financial plan for a business. Budgets typically include projections of cash inflows and outflows, as well as expected revenues and expenses. Budgets can be used to identify potential cash shortfalls and plan for unexpected expenses.

Implementing effective cash flow management

Implementing effective cash flow management involves several steps. The first step is to create a cash flow statement. This involves tracking all cash inflows and outflows, including sales revenue, expenses, and investments. Cash flow statements should be prepared on a regular basis, such as monthly or quarterly, to ensure that businesses have an accurate picture of their cash position.

The second step is to identify potential cash shortfalls. This involves analysing the cash flow statement and identifying periods where cash inflows are lower than cash outflows. This can help businesses anticipate potential cash shortages and take steps to manage their cash flow during these periods.

The third step is to manage accounts receivable and accounts payable. This involves tracking invoices and payments, following up on overdue payments, and negotiating payment terms with suppliers and creditors. Effective accounts receivable and accounts payable management can help businesses maintain their cash flow by ensuring that payments are received and made on time.

The fourth step is to manage inventory levels. This involves forecasting demand, tracking inventory levels, and ordering inventory as needed. Effective inventory management can help businesses maintain their cash flow by ensuring that they have enough inventory to meet demand without tying up too much cash in excess inventory.

The fifth step is to create a budget. This involves creating a financial plan that includes projections of cash inflows and outflows as well as expected revenues and expenses. Budgets can help businesses identify potential cash shortfalls and plan for unexpected expenses.

The sixth step is to monitor cash flow regularly. This involves reviewing cash flow statements on a regular basis, such as monthly or quarterly, and adjusting cash flow management strategies as needed. By monitoring cash flow regularly, businesses can identify areas where they can improve their cash flow management and make informed financial decisions.

IV. Human Resource Management

Human Resource Management (HRM) is a vital function of business management that is focused on managing and developing employees within an organization. HRM is concerned with recruiting, hiring, training, managing, and retaining employees, as well as creating policies and procedures that promote a positive work environment and support the company's overall objectives.

The primary responsibilities of HRM include:

1. Recruitment and selection: HRM is responsible for attracting, recruiting, and selecting the right talent for the organization. This involves job analysis, job design, the development of selection criteria, and the actual recruitment process.

2. Compensation and benefits: HRM is responsible for creating and administering compensation and benefit programmes that are competitive and attractive to employees.

3. Employee relations: HRM is responsible for managing employee relations, including employee grievances, conflicts, and disciplinary actions.

4. Compliance: HRM is responsible for ensuring that the organisation is in compliance with all applicable employment laws and regulations.

Hiring and Training Employees

Hiring and training employees are essential functions of human resource management (HRM). These functions are critical to the success of any organization, as they help to ensure that the right people are hired for the right jobs and that they are trained and developed to perform those jobs effectively.

Hiring employees typically involves the following steps:

1. Job analysis: HRM first analyse the job and determines the key responsibilities, duties and qualifications needed for the position. This information is used to develop a job description and job specification.

2. Sourcing candidates: Once the job description and specification have been developed, HRM sources candidates through a variety of channels, such as job boards, social media, and employee referrals.

3. Screening and selection: HRM then screens and selects the most qualified candidates based on their resumes, interviews, and references.

4. Job offer and acceptance: Finally, HRM extends a job offer to the selected candidate, and the candidate accepts the offer.

Training and development of employees are also critical to the success of any organization. The following steps are typically involved in the training and development process:

1. Needs assessment: HRM identifies the skills and knowledge that employees need to perform their jobs effectively and assesses any gaps in those skills and knowledge.

2. Training design: Based on the needs assessment, HRM designs a training programme that addresses the identified gaps in skills and knowledge.

3. Training delivery: HRM then delivers the training programme to employees, which may involve a variety of methods such as on-the-job training, classroom training, online training, or a combination of these methods.

4. Evaluation: Finally, HRM evaluates the effectiveness of the training program and determines if it has achieved its intended objectives. Any necessary adjustments or improvements are made to the programme based on the evaluation results.

Performance Management

Performance management is a key function of human resource management (HRM) that is concerned with creating a work environment where employees can excel and supporting the achievement of organisational goals and objectives. Performance management involves a range of activities, including setting performance expectations, evaluating employee performance, providing feedback and coaching, identifying performance improvement opportunities, and recognising and rewarding high-performing employees.

One of the key aspects of performance management is setting clear expectations for employee performance. This involves outlining specific objectives and targets that align with the organization's overall goals and objectives. When employees understand what is expected of them, they are better equipped to perform their job duties effectively and contribute to the organization's success.

Another critical aspect of performance management is the evaluation of employee performance. HRM assesses employee performance based on predetermined performance metrics and criteria, which may include factors such as productivity, quality of work, customer service, and teamwork. HRM may use a variety of tools to evaluate employee performance, including self-evaluation, 360-degree feedback, and supervisor feedback.

Feedback and coaching are also essential components of performance management. HRM provides employees with regular feedback on their performance, highlighting areas where they are excelling and areas where they need to improve. HRM may also provide coaching and guidance to employees to help them develop their skills and improve their performance. By providing employees with the support they need to succeed, HRM can create a culture of high performance and foster employee engagement and job satisfaction.

Performance improvement is another critical component of performance management. HRM works with employees to identify performance improvement opportunities and develop plans to improve their performance. This may involve additional training, coaching, or support from the organization. By helping employees improve their performance, HRM can support the achievement of organisational goals and improve overall productivity and efficiency.

Finally, recognition and reward are important components of performance management. HRM recognises and rewards employees who perform well, creating a culture of high performance and motivating employees to continue to excel. Recognition and reward programmes can include bonuses, promotions, public recognition, and other incentives that help reinforce the importance of performance excellence within the organization.

Employee Retention and Motivation

Employee retention and motivation are critical aspects of human resource management (HRM) that are essential to creating a positive and productive workplace. Employee retention refers to the ability of an organisation to retain its employees over time, while employee motivation refers to the factors that drive employee engagement, job satisfaction, and productivity.

One of the most effective ways to improve employee retention is to create a positive and supportive work environment. This involves developing a culture that values and supports employees, provides opportunities for professional development, and offers competitive compensation and benefits. HRM can also support employee retention by fostering open communication, recognising and rewarding employee achievements, and offering opportunities for advancement and growth within the organization.

Employee motivation is also essential to creating a productive and engaged workforce. Motivated employees are more likely to be committed to their work, take initiative, and contribute to the overall success of the organization. HRM can support employee motivation by providing employees with meaningful and challenging work, offering opportunities for growth and development, recognising and rewarding good performance, and fostering a positive and supportive work environment.

In addition to these strategies, HRM can also use a range of other tools and techniques to support employee retention and motivation. For example, HRM can conduct regular surveys and feedback sessions to gather employee opinions and ideas and use this information to make improvements to the work environment and the employee experience. HRM can also offer training and development programmes to help employees acquire new skills and advance their careers within the organization.

V. Operations Management

Operation management is the field of business management that is concerned with designing, controlling, and improving the production and delivery of goods and services. It involves the planning, organizing, and controlling of all aspects of the production process, from sourcing raw materials to delivering finished products to customers.

The primary goal of operation management is to ensure that a company's operations are efficient, effective, and productive. This involves optimising the use of resources, including people, machines, and materials, to maximise output and minimise waste.

Process improvement and optimization

Process improvement and optimization are key aspects of operation management. These practices are aimed at increasing efficiency, reducing waste, and improving the overall effectiveness of a company's production processes.

Process improvement involves analysing the current processes and identifying opportunities for improvement. This can involve analysing the steps involved in producing a product or delivering a service and looking for ways to streamline the process, eliminate waste, and reduce costs. For example, a manufacturing company might use process improvement to identify and eliminate bottlenecks in the production line or improve the quality control process to reduce defects.

Optimization involves fine-tuning the processes to achieve the best possible performance. This can involve analysing data to determine the optimal amount of resources needed for a given task or identifying the most efficient way to schedule production runs. For example, a company might optimise its inventory management process to ensure that it has the right amount of inventory on hand to meet demand without holding excess inventory that ties up cash.

Some common techniques used in process improvement and optimization include:

1. Lean management: A philosophy that seeks to eliminate waste and streamline processes by identifying and eliminating non-value-added activities.

2. Six Sigma: A methodology that uses statistical analysis to identify and eliminate defects in the production process.

3. Business process reengineering: A technique that involves redesigning entire processes to achieve significant improvements in efficiency and effectiveness.

4. Total quality management (TQM): a comprehensive approach to quality management that involves a focus on continuous improvement, customer satisfaction, and teamwork.

Supply Chain Management

Supply chain management (SCM) is the process of managing the flow of goods and services from the supplier to the end customer. It is a critical aspect of operations management that involves coordinating and optimising the movement of materials, information, and finances from the source of production to the point of consumption.

The primary goal of SCM is to ensure that the right products are delivered to the right customers at the right time and at the lowest possible cost. This involves managing the entire process, from sourcing raw materials and components through manufacturing and distribution to the final delivery of the product to the customer.

The key activities involved in SCM include:

1. Planning: This involves forecasting demand, developing production schedules, and managing inventory levels.

2. Sourcing: This involves identifying and selecting suppliers, negotiating contracts, and managing relationships with suppliers.

3. Manufacturing: This involves coordinating the production process, managing quality control, and optimising the use of resources.

4. Logistics: This involves managing the transportation and storage of goods, including scheduling shipments, managing inventory, and coordinating with transportation providers.

5. Delivery: This involves managing the delivery of goods to the end customer, including managing orders, tracking shipments, and managing returns.

Some common techniques used in SCM include:

1. Just-in-time (JIT): A philosophy that aims to reduce inventory levels by only ordering and receiving materials when they are needed for production.

2. Vendor-managed inventory (VMI): A technique that involves the supplier managing the inventory levels of the customer.

3. Cross-docking: A technique that involves transferring goods directly from inbound trucks to outbound trucks, minimising the need for storage.

4. Collaborative planning, forecasting, and replenishment (CPFR): A process that involves sharing information between the supplier and the customer to improve planning and reduce costs.

Quality Control

Quality control is a critical aspect of operations management that involves monitoring and verifying the quality of products or services produced by a company. The primary goal of quality control is to ensure that products or services meet the desired level of quality and are free from defects. This is important because defects can lead to customer dissatisfaction, reduced sales, and increased costs due to the need for repairs, rework, or returns. Quality control involves a range of activities such as inspection, testing, statistical process control, quality audits, and continuous improvement.

One of the key benefits of quality control is improved product or service quality. Quality control ensures that products or services meet the required level of quality, reducing the risk of defects and improving customer satisfaction. When customers receive products or services that meet their needs and expectations, they are more likely to be satisfied and loyal to the company. In contrast, defects can lead to customer dissatisfaction and lost sales, as well as damage to the company's reputation.

Another benefit of quality control is reduced costs. By reducing the number of defects and improving the efficiency of the production process, quality control can help reduce costs and improve profitability. This is because defects can be costly to repair, and they can also lead to wasted materials, additional labour, and lost productivity. Quality control can help identify the root causes of defects and eliminate them, reducing the need for repairs, rework, or returns. In addition, by improving the efficiency of the production process, quality control can help reduce waste and increase productivity.

Finally, quality control can help improve customer satisfaction. Quality control ensures that products or services meet the needs and expectations of customers, improving their overall satisfaction with the company. This can lead to increased sales, repeat business, and positive word-of-mouth advertising, all of which can contribute to the company's success.

VI. Marketing and Sales Management

Marketing management and sales management are two distinct yet closely related functions that are essential to the success of any business.

Marketing management is the process of planning, organizing, directing, and controlling the activities of a company's marketing function. Its primary objective is to identify and meet the needs and wants of customers through the creation, promotion, and distribution of products and services. This involves a range of activities, including market research, product development, pricing, advertising and promotions, and distribution management.

Effective marketing management requires a deep understanding of customer needs and preferences, market trends, and the competitive landscape. Market research plays a critical role in this process, as it helps companies identify customer needs, assess the competition, and develop effective marketing strategies. Marketing managers are responsible for analysing market data, developing marketing plans, and implementing tactics to achieve the company's marketing objectives.

Sales management, on the other hand, is the process of planning, directing, and controlling the personal selling activities of a company to achieve sales objectives. This includes managing the sales force, designing and implementing sales strategies and tactics, and setting sales targets and goals.

Sales management is closely related to marketing management, as the sales function is responsible for converting the demand created by the marketing function into actual sales. Sales managers work closely with marketing managers to develop sales strategies that align with the overall marketing plan and ensure that sales activities are consistent with the company's overall goals and objectives.

Effective sales management requires a range of skills, including communication, leadership, and strategic planning. Sales managers must be able to motivate and train their sales teams, analyse sales data, develop sales forecasts, and identify opportunities for growth. They must also be able to work closely with other departments within the company, such as marketing, finance, and operations, to ensure that sales activities are aligned with the company's overall strategy.

Developing a Market Plan

Developing a marketing plan is the process of creating a comprehensive document that outlines a company's marketing strategies and tactics to achieve its business goals. It involves analysing the market, identifying target audiences, setting goals and objectives, and developing a roadmap for how to achieve them.

The first step in developing a marketing plan is to conduct a situational analysis. This involves analysing the current state of the market, including market trends, competitor analysis, and the company's strengths, weaknesses, opportunities, and threats (SWOT analysis). This analysis helps identify market gaps and potential opportunities.

The second step is to define the target audience. Identifying and understanding the needs and preferences of the target audience is essential to the success of the marketing plan. This involves identifying the demographics, psychographics, and behaviour of potential customers as well as understanding their buying patterns.

The third step is to set specific and measurable marketing objectives. These objectives should be aligned with the company's overall goals and be achievable within a specific timeframe. The objectives should be specific and measurable to ensure that the company can track progress towards achieving its goals.

Once the marketing objectives have been established, the fourth step is to develop marketing strategies. The marketing strategies should be designed to guide the company's marketing activities and achieve the marketing objectives. These strategies may include product development, pricing, promotion, and distribution strategies.

The final step is to determine the specific tactics that will be used to implement the marketing strategies. These tactics may include advertising, direct marketing, public relations, sales promotions, and personal selling. The tactics should be consistent with the overall marketing strategies and tailored to the specific needs and preferences of the target audience.

Conducting market research

Conducting market research is a crucial process that businesses must undertake to understand their target market and create effective marketing strategies. The research process involves gathering and analysing data related to a specific market or industry. The insights gained through market research provide businesses with valuable information on customer preferences, needs, and behaviours, as well as on the competition and overall market trends. Market research helps businesses make informed decisions about their products, services, and marketing strategies, which ultimately lead to a competitive advantage in the marketplace.

The first step in conducting market research is to define the research objectives. This involves identifying the information that is needed, why it is needed, and how it will be used. The research objectives are the foundation of the research process, and all subsequent decisions are based on these objectives. Once the research objectives are defined, the next step is to identify the target audience for the research. This includes defining the demographics, psychographics, and behaviours of the people who will be surveyed or studied.

After identifying the target audience, the next step is to select the most appropriate research methodologies based on the research objectives and the target audience. The selected methodologies may include surveys, focus groups, in-depth interviews, or observational studies. The data collection process involves executing the selected research methodologies. This may involve distributing surveys, conducting focus groups, or observing behaviour in a natural setting.

Once the data has been collected, it must be analysed to draw meaningful conclusions. The data analysis involves summarising the data, identifying patterns, and drawing conclusions based on the research objectives. Finally, based on the data analysis, conclusions are drawn and recommendations are made. These recommendations may include suggestions for product development, pricing, promotion, and distribution strategies.

Sales Forecast and Analysis

Sales forecasting and analysis is the process of estimating future sales revenue for a business. It involves analysing historical sales data, market trends, and other factors that may impact future sales to make accurate predictions about future revenue. Sales forecasting and analysis are essential for businesses of all sizes, as they help them plan and make informed decisions about sales strategies, production, staffing, and budgeting.

The first step in sales forecasting and analysis is to gather historical sales data. This data provides a baseline for predicting future sales and can be used to identify trends and patterns. Once the historical sales data is collected, the next step is to analyse it to identify factors that may impact future sales. This may include changes in the economy, customer behaviour, and competition.

The next step is to identify market trends that may impact future sales. This involves analysing market research data, monitoring consumer trends, and studying the competition. By understanding these factors, businesses can predict how changes in the market may impact their sales.

Once the historical sales data and market trends have been analyzed, the next step is to develop a sales forecast. This involves using the data to make accurate predictions about future sales revenue. There are several methods for developing a sales forecast, including trend analysis, regression analysis, and the subjective or expert opinion method. The method used will depend on the business and the data available.

After the sales forecast has been developed, the next step is to analyse the forecast to determine its accuracy. This involves comparing the forecast to actual sales revenue over time. By analysing the accuracy of the forecast, businesses can identify areas for improvement and refine their sales forecasting and analysis methods.

VII. Risk Management

Risk management in managing a business involves identifying, assessing, and prioritising risks that could potentially impact the organization's ability to achieve its objectives. The objective of risk management is to reduce the likelihood and severity of negative events and increase the likelihood and magnitude of positive outcomes.

Identifying and Assessing Risk

Identifying and assessing risks are the first steps in risk management. These steps involve analysing the internal and external factors that could impact a business and evaluating the likelihood and potential impact of each risk.

Here is a breakdown of how identifying and assessing risks can be done:

1. **Identify Risks:** The first step is to identify potential risks that could impact the business. These risks can be classified into different categories, such as strategic, financial, operational, legal, and reputational risks. The identification of risks can be done through brainstorming sessions, reviewing historical data and industry trends, and consulting with experts in the relevant fields.

2. **Assess Risks:** Once potential risks are identified, they need to be assessed to determine the likelihood and potential impact of each risk. This involves analysing the frequency of occurrence and the severity of the impact of each risk. This process allows businesses to prioritise risks based on their potential impact on the organization.

A common tool used in this step is a risk matrix, which is a graphical representation of the likelihood and impact of risks.

3. Determine Risk Tolerance: After assessing risks, the business needs to determine its risk tolerance. Risk tolerance is the level of risk that the organisation is willing to accept. This is a subjective decision that depends on the organization's goals, values, and available resources.

By identifying and assessing risks, businesses can take proactive measures to manage those that could potentially impact their operations. This can help to minimise the negative impact of risks and improve the overall success and sustainability of the organization.

Developing a risk management plan

A risk management plan outlines how the organisation will identify, assess, and respond to risks. This plan should be based on the identified and assessed risks and the organization's risk tolerance level. Here are some steps for developing a risk management plan:

1. Develop risk response strategies: Based on the assessed risks, the organisation should develop risk response strategies. These strategies should be designed to mitigate, transfer, avoid, or accept the risks. The risk response strategies should be aligned with the organization's risk tolerance level.

2. Implement Risk Response Strategies: After developing the risk response strategies, the organisation should implement them. This involves assigning responsibilities for each strategy, providing the necessary resources and training, and establishing a system for monitoring and controlling the risks.

3. Monitor and Review: The organisation should monitor and review the risk management plan regularly to ensure that it is effective in managing the identified risks. This involves reviewing the plan periodically, updating the plan when necessary, and ensuring that the risk management strategies are still effective in mitigating the identified risks.

A well-developed risk management plan can help organisations manage risks and improve their overall success and sustainability. The plan should be flexible and responsive to changes in the internal and external environment, and it should be reviewed and updated regularly to ensure its effectiveness.

Implementation of risk management strategies

Implementing risk management strategies involves identifying, assessing, and prioritising risks, then developing and executing strategies to manage those risks effectively.

Here are some steps to implement risk management strategies:

1. Establish risk management processes: Develop processes and procedures to implement the risk management strategies. Define roles and responsibilities and create a risk management plan.

2. Communicate risks and strategies: Communicate the risks and the strategies to the relevant stakeholders, including senior management, project teams, and other key stakeholders. Make sure everyone understands the risks and the strategies to manage them.

3. Monitor and review: Continuously monitor and review the effectiveness of the risk management strategies. Make adjustments as necessary to ensure they remain effective.

4. Incorporate risk management into decision-making: Incorporate risk management into decision-making processes to ensure risks are considered when making business decisions.

By implementing these steps, organisations can effectively manage risks and minimise the negative impact of those risks on their operations, projects, and processes.

VIII. *legal and regulatory compliance*

Legal and regulatory compliance in business management refers to the process of ensuring that a company operates within the legal and regulatory framework of the jurisdictions in which it operates. This includes adherence to laws, regulations, and other requirements set forth by local, state, and federal governments, as well as industry-specific standards.

Compliance is critical for companies as it helps them avoid legal penalties, fines, and reputational damage. It also helps ensure that a company operates in an ethical and responsible manner, which can enhance its reputation, attract investors and customers, and increase its overall success.

Legal and regulatory compliance involves a range of activities, such as monitoring changes in laws and regulations, training employees on compliance requirements, conducting audits and assessments, and implementing policies and procedures to ensure compliance. Companies may also work with legal or compliance experts to assist in ensuring they are meeting their obligations.

Some examples of areas where companies need to ensure compliance include data protection, workplace safety, financial reporting, labour and employment practices, and environmental regulations. By staying up-to-date on the relevant laws and regulations and implementing appropriate compliance measures, companies can operate effectively and responsibly in their industries.

Understanding Legal and Regulatory Requirements

Understanding legal and regulatory requirements is crucial for individuals and organisations to ensure compliance with the laws, regulations, and standards that are applicable to their activities. Failure to comply with legal and regulatory requirements can lead to legal penalties, fines, reputational damage, and other negative consequences.

To understand legal and regulatory requirements, individuals and organisations must first identify the laws, regulations, and standards that apply to their specific activities. This may involve conducting research and seeking guidance from legal or compliance experts to determine the relevant requirements.

Once the requirements have been identified, individuals and organisations must ensure they are meeting the requirements by implementing appropriate policies, procedures, and controls. This may include training employees on compliance requirements, monitoring compliance, and conducting audits and assessments to ensure ongoing compliance.

It is important to note that legal and regulatory requirements can vary depending on the industry, geographic location, and other factors. Therefore, individuals and organisations must stay up-to-date on changes to legal and regulatory requirements and adjust their compliance measures accordingly.

Finally, it is important to take a proactive approach to compliance by integrating compliance considerations into all aspects of an organization's activities. This may include embedding compliance into business processes, engaging with stakeholders on compliance issues, and seeking opportunities to continuously improve compliance measures.

Developing a Compliance Program

Developing a compliance programme is an essential part of ensuring that an organisation meets legal and regulatory requirements. An effective compliance programme should be tailored to the specific needs of the organization and should be designed to ensure that all employees understand their responsibilities and obligations under applicable laws and regulations. Here are some key steps to consider when developing a compliance program:

1. **Conduct a risk assessment**: A risk assessment can help identify areas of the organisation that are most vulnerable to compliance risks. This can include evaluating potential legal and regulatory violations, ethical breaches, and reputational risks.

2. **Establish policies and procedures**: Policies and procedures should be established to ensure that all employees understand their responsibilities and obligations under applicable laws and regulations. These policies

should be clear and easily accessible, and they should be regularly reviewed and updated.

3. Implement Training Programs: A comprehensive training programme should be established to ensure that all employees understand their role in complying with legal and regulatory requirements. This can include both general compliance training as well as targeted training in areas of higher risk.

4. Create Reporting Channels: It is important to establish reporting channels that allow employees to report potential compliance violations without fear of retaliation. These channels should be easily accessible and confidential.

5. Monitor Compliance: Ongoing monitoring and auditing of the compliance programme can help ensure that it remains effective and relevant. This can include conducting regular internal audits, external assessments, and performance reviews.

6. Respond to Violations: It is important to establish procedures for responding to compliance violations when they occur. This can include investigations, corrective action, and disciplinary measures as necessary.

7.Continuously Improve: Finally, it is important to continuously improve the compliance programme by learning from past experiences, monitoring trends, and adapting to changes in laws and regulations.

By following these steps, organisations can develop a compliance programme that helps ensure compliance with legal and regulatory requirements, reduces risk, and enhances the organization's reputation.

IX. Conclusion

Managing a business requires a comprehensive and integrated approach that covers various aspects of operations. Effective business management is essential for achieving business goals and objectives, maximising profitability, and ensuring sustainability in the long run. The establishment of a business management framework, financial management, human resource management, operations management, marketing and sales management, risk management, and legal and regulatory compliance are all key areas of focus in business management.

The success of a business depends on its ability to adapt to changing market trends and remain competitive. Business owners and managers must keep up with the latest trends and best practices in business management to achieve their goals and objectives. By implementing appropriate strategies, businesses can improve their overall performance, mitigate risks, and stay ahead of the competition.

Overall, effective business management is critical to the success and sustainability of a business. Business owners and managers who prioritise business management and take the necessary steps to improve their operations will be better positioned to achieve their goals and objectives, maximise profitability, and ensure long-term success.

Overcoming Obstacles and Coping with failure

I. Introduction

The road to success in business is rarely a smooth one. Along the way, entrepreneurs and business owners encounter numerous obstacles and setbacks that can test their resilience and determination. From failed ventures to unexpected market shifts, these challenges can be difficult to navigate and can leave even the most seasoned business professionals feeling discouraged.

However, it's important to recognize that setbacks and failures are an inevitable part of any business journey. The most successful entrepreneurs and business owners are those who are able to overcome obstacles and use failure as a stepping stone to greater success.

In this chapter, we will explore the common obstacles and challenges that business owners face, as well as strategies for overcoming them. We'll also examine the importance of resilience, perseverance, and adaptability in the face of failure, and provide tips for coping with disappointment and moving forward in a productive and positive way.

Whether you're just starting out in business or are a seasoned professional, the insights and strategies presented in this chapter will help you overcome obstacles and find success in even the most challenging of circumstances.

Brief Overview

This chapter on "Overcoming Obstacles and Coping with Failure in Business" provides a comprehensive guide for entrepreneurs and business owners looking to develop resilience and overcome common obstacles and challenges that arise in business. It explores the importance of resilience, perseverance, and adaptability when dealing with obstacles and failures, and provides tips for coping with disappointment and moving forward in a positive and productive way.

The chapter covers a range of topics, including the inevitability of obstacles and challenges in business, the value of failure as a learning opportunity, common obstacles such as competition and cash flow, and strategies for overcoming these challenges. It also delves into the importance of developing a growth mindset and using failure as a stepping stone to greater success.

Throughout the chapter, readers will find practical advice and strategies for overcoming obstacles and developing the skills necessary to thrive in the fast-paced and competitive world of business. Whether you're just starting out in business or are a seasoned professional, the insights and strategies presented in this chapter will help you overcome obstacles and find success in even the most challenging of circumstances.

Importance of overcoming obstacles and coping with failure in business

Overcoming obstacles and coping with failure are critical skills for success in business. No matter how carefully you plan or how talented you are, obstacles and challenges are a natural part of any business journey. Being able to overcome these hurdles is essential to achieving your goals and building a successful business. However, it's important to recognize that failure is not always a bad thing. In fact, failure is a valuable learning opportunity that can help you grow and improve your business.

One of the biggest obstacles that business owners face is competition. In today's global marketplace, competition is fierce and constantly evolving. However, by developing a strong understanding of your competition and your target audience, you can position your business for success. This may involve making strategic investments in marketing and advertising, developing unique products or services that stand out from the competition, or simply focusing on providing the best possible customer service to your clients.

Another common obstacle in business is cash flow. Many businesses struggle to maintain consistent cash flow, particularly in the early stages of growth. This can make it difficult to cover expenses, invest in new products or services, or pay employees. However, by developing a solid financial plan and carefully managing your expenses, you can avoid cash flow issues and ensure that your business remains profitable in the long run.

Overcoming obstacles and coping with failure requires resilience, perseverance, and adaptability - all traits that are highly valued in the business world. By developing these skills, you'll be better equipped to handle whatever challenges come your way and emerge stronger and more successful as a result. It's important to approach obstacles and failures with a growth mindset, viewing them as opportunities for learning and improvement rather than as setbacks or roadblocks.

Ultimately, the ability to overcome obstacles and cope with failure is what separates successful entrepreneurs and business owners from those who give up at the first sign of difficulty. By embracing challenges and developing the skills necessary to navigate them, you can position yourself and your business for long-term success.

II. Types of Obstacle in Business

An obstacle in business refers to any factor or challenge that may impede a company's ability to achieve its goals or hinder its overall success. These obstacles can come in various forms and can impact different areas of the business, such as operations, marketing, finances, and management. Overcoming these obstacles requires careful planning, adaptability, and persistence. There are several types of Obstacle in Business:

1.Financial Obstacles

Financial obstacles are one of the most common challenges that businesses face. These obstacles can arise due to various factors, such as limited cash flow, unexpected expenses, and difficulty securing funding. Financial obstacles can affect all areas of a business, including operations, marketing, and expansion. Here are some common financial obstacles that businesses may face:

a) Limited cash flow: A company's cash flow refers to the money it has available to cover its day-to-day expenses.

Limited cash flow can arise due to slow-paying customers, uncollected debts, or unexpected expenses. This can lead to difficulty paying bills, salaries, or purchasing necessary inventory or equipment.

b) Poor credit: If a business has poor credit, it can be challenging to secure loans or lines of credit to cover expenses or invest in growth opportunities.

c) High expenses: Businesses that have high expenses may struggle to maintain profitability, especially if they are unable to pass those expenses onto customers. High expenses can arise due to factors such as high rent, utility bills, and labor costs.

d) Tax and regulatory compliance: Tax and regulatory compliance can be time-consuming and expensive to implement, especially for small businesses that may not have dedicated accounting or legal departments.

e) Lack of investment: A lack of investment can make it challenging for a business to expand, invest in new technology, or take advantage of new growth opportunities.

To overcome financial obstacles, businesses may need to consider strategies such as cutting costs, improving cash flow management, seeking investment or financing, renegotiating payment terms with vendors, or increasing sales and revenue through marketing or sales strategies. It's essential for businesses to monitor their finances regularly and be proactive in addressing financial challenges as they arise.

2. Personnel Obstacles

Personnel obstacles in business refer to challenges related to managing employees, including hiring, retaining, and developing talent. These obstacles can have a significant impact on a company's performance, productivity, and profitability. Some common personnel obstacles in business include:

a) Recruitment and Retention: Finding and hiring the right employees can be challenging, especially in a competitive job market. Once you have hired good employees, retaining them can also be a challenge, as employees may be lured away by better job opportunities or dissatisfied with their current work conditions.

b) Training and Development: To keep employees engaged and motivated, businesses need to provide them with opportunities to learn and grow. However, training and development programs can be time-consuming and expensive, and ensuring that they are effective can be a challenge.

c) Performance Management: Managing employee performance is essential to achieving business goals. However, performance management can be a sensitive issue, and managers need to be skilled in providing feedback, setting goals, and motivating employees.

d) Workplace Diversity and Inclusion: Companies that lack diversity and inclusivity may struggle to attract and retain employees, and may miss out on the benefits of a diverse workforce. Creating an inclusive work environment requires ongoing effort and commitment from leaders and employees alike.

e) Employee Conflict: Workplace conflicts can arise due to differences in personalities, communication styles, or work styles. Managing conflicts effectively is essential to maintaining a healthy work environment and preventing disruptions to business operations.

3.Legal Obstacles

Legal obstacles in business refer to challenges related to complying with laws, regulations, and legal requirements. Failure to comply with these requirements can result in significant legal and financial consequences, including fines, lawsuits, and damage to a company's reputation. Some common legal obstacles in business include:

a) Regulatory Compliance: Companies are subject to a range of regulations and requirements at the local, state, and federal levels, which can vary depending on the industry. Ensuring that the company complies with these regulations can be complex and time-consuming.

b) Intellectual Property Protection: Protecting intellectual property, such as trademarks, patents, and copyrights, is critical for many businesses. Failing to protect intellectual property can result in lost revenue, legal disputes, and damage to the company's brand.

c) Contract Law: Contracts are a vital aspect of many business operations, and disputes can arise over issues such as breach of contract, non-performance, and interpretation. Ensuring that contracts are legally sound and enforceable is essential to preventing legal disputes.

d) Employment Law: Businesses must comply with a range of employment laws, including those related to hiring, discrimination, harassment, and termination. Failure to comply with these laws can result in legal action and damage to the company's reputation.

e) Consumer Protection Laws: Consumer protection laws regulate how businesses can advertise, market, and sell their products and services. Violations of these laws can result in legal action, fines, and damage to the company's reputation.

4. Technological Obstacles

Technological obstacles in business refer to challenges related to adopting, implementing, and using technology effectively. In today's increasingly digital business environment, technology can play a significant role in a company's success, and failing to keep up with technological advancements can put businesses at a disadvantage. Some common technological obstacles in business include:

a) Legacy Systems: Legacy systems are outdated technology that may be difficult to integrate with newer technology. These systems can limit a company's ability to adopt new technology, and may make it challenging to keep up with industry standards.

b) Cybersecurity: Cybersecurity threats, such as data breaches, hacks, and malware, pose a significant risk to businesses. Implementing effective cybersecurity measures, such as firewalls, encryption, and employee training, is critical to protecting sensitive business information and maintaining customer trust.

c) Data Management: Businesses must manage and analyze vast amounts of data to make informed decisions. However, data management can be complex and time-consuming, and companies may struggle to effectively collect, store, and analyze data.

d) Integration: Implementing new technology can be challenging, particularly if it needs to integrate with existing systems. Ensuring that new technology works seamlessly with existing systems is essential to maximizing its effectiveness.

e) Obsolescence: Technology is constantly evolving, and companies that fail to keep up with advancements may find themselves at a disadvantage. Obsolete technology can be costly to maintain, limit productivity, and reduce the competitiveness of a business.

5. Competition Obstacles

Competition obstacles in business refer to challenges related to competing with other businesses in the same industry or market. Competition is a fundamental aspect of business, and companies that fail to differentiate themselves from their competitors may struggle to attract and retain customers. Some common competition obstacles in business include:

a) Pricing: Pricing is a key factor in determining a company's competitiveness. Setting prices that are too high may drive customers to competitors, while setting prices too low may result in reduced profit margins.

b) Product Differentiation: Offering unique or differentiated products or services can help companies stand out from competitors. However, creating differentiated products can be expensive and time-consuming, and companies must be able to effectively communicate the value of their products to customers.

c) Marketing: Effective marketing is essential to attracting and retaining customers. However, standing out in a crowded marketplace can be a challenge, and companies must be able to effectively differentiate themselves from competitors in their marketing messages.

d) Customer Service: Providing excellent customer service is essential to building customer loyalty and standing out from competitors. However, providing high-quality customer service can be expensive and time-consuming, and companies must be able to balance the cost of providing customer service with the benefits of customer loyalty.

e) Supply Chain Management: Managing the supply chain can be a significant competitive advantage. Companies that are able to effectively manage their supply chains can reduce costs, improve efficiency, and offer better customer service. However, managing the supply chain can be complex, and companies must be able to effectively balance cost and efficiency.

III. Strategies for Overcoming Obstacles in Business

There are several strategies that can be helpful in overcoming obstacles in business. Here are some of them:

1. Developing a growth mindset:

Developing a growth mindset can be a powerful strategy for overcoming obstacles in business. Here are some steps you can take to develop a growth mindset:

a) Embrace challenges: Instead of shying away from challenges, view them as opportunities for growth and learning. See challenges as a chance to improve your skills, knowledge, and abilities.

b) Learn from failures: Failure is a natural part of business, and it's important to learn from your mistakes. Rather than viewing failure as a setback, look at it as a chance to learn and grow.

c) Cultivate resilience: Resilience is the ability to bounce back from setbacks and persevere in the face of challenges. To cultivate resilience, focus on building your inner strength and developing a positive mindset.

d) Seek out feedback: Feedback can be a valuable tool for growth and development. Seek out feedback from others and use it to improve your skills and abilities.

e) Continuously learn: The business world is constantly changing, and it's important to stay up-to-date with the latest trends and best practices. Continuously learning and seeking out new information can help you stay ahead of the curve and overcome obstacles with greater ease.

By developing a growth mindset, you can approach obstacles in business with a positive attitude and a willingness to learn and grow. This can help you overcome challenges and achieve greater success in your business endeavours.

2. Break down the problem

Breaking down the problem is a strategy for overcoming obstacles in business that involves breaking a complex problem into smaller, more manageable parts. Here are some steps you can take to implement this strategy:

a) **Define the problem:** The first step is to clearly define the problem you are facing. This involves identifying the specific challenge you are trying to overcome and understanding the impact it is having on your business.

b) **Break the problem down:** Once you have defined the problem, break it down into smaller, more manageable parts. This can help you identify the underlying causes of the problem and develop targeted solutions to address each one.

c) **Prioritize the parts:** Once you have broken the problem down, prioritize the parts based on their importance and impact on your business. This can help you focus your efforts on the most critical areas and achieve the greatest impact.

d) **Develop solutions:** With a clear understanding of the problem and its underlying causes, develop targeted solutions for each part. This may involve brainstorming, research, or consulting with experts in your field.

e) **Implement solutions:** Once you have developed your solutions, implement them one at a time, starting with the most critical part. This allows you to evaluate the effectiveness of each solution and make adjustments as needed.

By breaking down the problem into smaller parts, you can tackle each component with greater focus and efficiency. This can help you overcome obstacles in your business with greater ease and achieve your goals more effectively.

3. Find a Mentor or Advisor

Finding a mentor or advisor is a strategy for overcoming obstacles in business that involves seeking out the guidance and advice of a more experienced individual. Here are some steps you can take to implement this strategy:

a) Identify your needs: The first step is to identify the specific challenges or obstacles you are facing in your business. This can help you determine the type of mentor or advisor you need to seek out.

b) Look for potential mentors or advisors: Look for individuals in your industry or field who have experience and expertise in the areas where you need guidance. This may involve networking, attending industry events, or seeking out referrals from colleagues.

c) Reach out to potential mentors or advisors: Once you have identified potential mentors or advisors, reach out to them to introduce yourself and express your interest in learning from them. This may involve sending an email, making a phone call, or scheduling a meeting.

d) Be open to feedback and guidance: When working with a mentor or advisor, be open to their feedback and guidance. Listen carefully to their advice and consider their perspective on your business challenges.

e) Build a relationship: Building a strong relationship with your mentor or advisor is key to making the most of this strategy. Make time for regular meetings or check-ins, and keep them updated on your progress.

By seeking out the guidance and advice of a mentor or advisor, you can benefit from their experience and expertise, and gain valuable insights into how to overcome obstacles in your business. This can help you develop new skills and knowledge, improve your decision-making, and ultimately achieve greater success in your business endeavours

4. Experiment with different solutions

Experimenting with different solutions is a strategy in business that involves trying out different approaches to see what works best. Here are some steps you can take to implement this strategy:

a) Identify the problem: The first step is to clearly identify the problem you are trying to solve. This involves understanding the root cause of the obstacle and the impact it is having on your business.

b) Brainstorm potential solutions: Once you have identified the problem, brainstorm a list of potential solutions. This may involve consulting with colleagues or industry experts, researching best practices, or drawing on your own experience.

c) Choose a solution to test: Select one of the potential solutions from your list and develop a plan to test it. This may involve setting up a pilot program, conducting a trial run, or implementing the solution on a small scale.

d) Monitor and evaluate the results: As you test the solution, monitor the results and evaluate its effectiveness.

This may involve collecting data, gathering feedback from stakeholders, or conducting surveys or other forms of research.

e) Refine or pivot as needed: Based on the results of your testing, refine or pivot the solution as needed. This may involve tweaking the approach, trying a different solution from your list, or developing a new solution based on your findings.

f) Repeat the process: Once you have refined the solution, test it again and continue to monitor and evaluate its effectiveness. Repeat this process until you find a solution that works well for your business.

By experimenting with different solutions, you can find the approach that works best for your business and overcome obstacles with greater ease. This can help you develop new skills and knowledge, improve your decision-making, and ultimately achieve greater success in your business endeavours.

5. Stay positive and focused

Staying positive and focused is a strategy in business that involves maintaining a positive attitude and staying focused on your goals, even in the face of challenges. Here are some steps you can take to implement this strategy:

a) Acknowledge the challenge: The first step is to acknowledge the obstacle or challenge you are facing. This involves accepting that the situation is difficult and may require a lot of effort and persistence to overcome.

b) Keep your eye on the goal: While you are working to overcome the obstacle, keep your eye on your long-term goals. This can help you stay focused and motivated, even when the going gets tough.

c) Stay positive: Maintain a positive attitude throughout the process. Focus on the progress you are making, rather than the obstacles that remain. Celebrate small successes and use them as motivation to keep moving forward.

d) Surround yourself with support: Seek out the support of colleagues, friends, or family members who can encourage and motivate you. This may involve joining a support group, attending industry events, or simply reaching out to people in your network.

e) Take care of yourself: It's important to take care of yourself throughout the process. This may involve getting enough sleep, eating a healthy diet, exercising regularly, and taking breaks when you need them.

6. Seek out Resources and Reports

Seeking out resources and reports is a strategy in business that involves looking for information and tools that can help you better understand and address the challenges you are facing. Here are some steps you can take to implement this strategy:

a) Identify the obstacle: The first step is to identify the obstacle or challenge you are facing. This involves understanding the root cause of the problem and the impact it is having on your business.

b) Research resources: Once you have identified the challenge, research the resources available to you. This may involve looking for industry reports, case studies, online forums, or other resources that can help you better understand the issue.

c) Gather information: Collect as much information as you can about the challenge and the available resources. This may involve reading reports, attending webinars, or talking to experts in the field.

d) Analyze the information: Once you have gathered information, analyze it to gain insights into how to address the challenge. Look for patterns or trends that can help you better understand the issue, and identify best practices or strategies that have been successful in similar situations.

e) Develop an action plan: Based on your analysis, develop an action plan for addressing the challenge. This may involve implementing a new process, hiring additional staff, or seeking out additional resources or support.

f) Implement the plan: Put your action plan into action and monitor the results. Use data and feedback to adjust your approach as needed.

IV. Coping With Failures in Business

Coping with failure in business refers to the strategies, attitudes, and behaviours that entrepreneurs and business leaders adopt to manage the disappointment, setbacks, and challenges that arise from their ventures not meeting their goals or objectives. Failure in business is a common experience, and it can take different forms, such as the failure of a business idea, product, project, or a whole enterprise. Coping with failure is an essential skill for business leaders to develop because it can help them learn from their mistakes, become more resilient, and improve their chances of future success.

The psychological impact of failure: The psychological impact of failure can be significant and varied, as it can affect individuals differently. Failure can trigger negative emotions and thought patterns that can be difficult to manage. One of the most common psychological impacts of failure is self-doubt and negative self-talk. When someone experiences failure, it can erode their confidence and self-esteem, leading to feelings of self-doubt and negative self-talk. This can create a cycle of negative thoughts that can be hard to break, and it can interfere with their ability to take on new challenges in the future.

Another psychological impact of failure is stress and anxiety. When someone experiences failure, it can lead to stress, which can result in physical and mental health problems if not managed. Stress can manifest in the form of anxiety, insomnia, or physical symptoms such as headaches or digestive issues. The stress and anxiety associated with failure can be overwhelming, and it's important for individuals to manage these feelings to prevent them from becoming a long-term issue.

Depression is another psychological impact of failure. Failure can trigger feelings of depression, particularly if the individual feels that the failure is a reflection of their worth as a person. These feelings of depression can be severe and can impact an individual's ability to function in their personal and professional lives. Fear of failure or rejection is another psychological impact of failure. When someone experiences failure, it can create a fear of rejection or failure, which can lead to avoidance behaviours, such as not pursuing new opportunities or taking risks.

Failure can also cause a loss of motivation. When someone experiences failure, it can cause a loss of motivation, particularly if the individual feels that their efforts have not been rewarded. This can result in a lack of enthusiasm for future projects or goals. Finally, guilt or shame can be another psychological impact of failure. When someone experiences failure, it can trigger feelings of guilt or shame, particularly if the individual feels responsible for the failure. These feelings can be difficult to manage and can interfere with the ability to move forward.

In coping with failure, it's important to recognize and manage the psychological impacts that failure can have. Strategies such as seeking support from others, reframing the failure as a learning opportunity, and focusing on the positive aspects of the experience can help individuals manage the psychological impacts of failure and move forward with renewed confidence and resilience. It's important to recognize that failure is a natural part of the learning process and can provide valuable lessons that can be applied to future endeavours.

Strategies for Bouncing Back from failure: Bouncing back from failure can be challenging, but it's essential for personal and professional growth. Here are some strategies that can help individuals bounce back from failure:

a) Reframe the failure as a learning opportunity: Instead of dwelling on the negative aspects of the failure, try to focus on the lessons that can be learned from it. Analyze what went wrong and what could have been done differently. This can help individuals avoid making the same mistakes in the future.

b) Seek support from others: Talk to trusted friends, family members, or colleagues about the failure. Their support and encouragement can be invaluable in helping individuals bounce back from failure. They can provide a fresh perspective and offer advice and guidance.

c) Practice self-compassion: Be kind and understanding towards yourself. Failure can be tough on an individual's self-esteem, and it's essential to practice self-compassion. This means treating oneself with the same care and kindness as one would treat a good friend.

d) Set realistic goals: Setting small, achievable goals can help individuals build confidence and motivation. This can be particularly helpful after a failure, as it can help individuals regain a sense of control and accomplishment.

e) Take care of physical and mental health: Failure can cause stress and anxiety, which can impact an individual's physical and mental health. It's important to prioritize self-care, such as getting enough sleep, eating well, and engaging in activities that promote relaxation and well-being.

f) Try again: Finally, don't be afraid to try again. Failure is a natural part of the learning process, and it's important to take risks and try new things. Every failure provides an opportunity to learn and grow, and the experience gained can be applied to future endeavours.

Bouncing back from failure is not always easy, but with the right mindset and strategies, it's possible to move forward and achieve success. By practising self-compassion, seeking support from others, setting realistic goals, taking care of physical and mental health, and reframing failure as a learning opportunity, individuals can bounce back from failure and achieve personal and professional growth.

Learning from failure and applying the lesson

Learning from failure is an essential step towards personal and professional growth. To learn from failure, it's important to take time to reflect on what went wrong and what could have been done differently. This reflection can be challenging, as it may involve facing uncomfortable truths and acknowledging mistakes. However, it's a critical step towards understanding the root cause of the failure and identifying strategies for improvement.

Once the reflection process is complete, it's important to focus on the lessons learned. This means identifying specific actions that can be taken to prevent the same mistake from happening again. For example, if the failure was due to poor communication, the lesson learned may be to improve communication skills, such as active listening and clear articulation.

Applying the lessons learned is the final step in the process. This means taking action to implement the strategies identified during the reflection process. This may involve seeking feedback from others, taking courses or training to improve skills, or developing new habits or routines. It's important to remember that applying the lessons learned may involve taking risks and trying new things. However, it's through these experiences that individuals can grow and develop.

Learning from failure is not always easy, but it's an essential step towards personal and professional growth. By taking time to reflect on the failure, focusing on the lessons learned, and applying these lessons, individuals can develop resilience, build confidence, and achieve success. Ultimately, failure can be a valuable opportunity for growth and improvement, and it's important to embrace it as a natural part of the learning process.

Reframing failure as an opportunity for growth

Reframing failure as an opportunity for growth is a powerful mindset shift that can help individuals develop resilience, build confidence, and achieve success. Instead of seeing failure as a negative experience, it's possible to view it as a chance to learn and improve. This mindset shift can be challenging, as it may involve re-evaluating deeply ingrained beliefs about success and failure. However, with practice, it's possible to develop a growth mindset that sees failure as a natural part of the learning process.

To reframe failure as an opportunity for growth, it's important to focus on the lessons learned from the experience. This means asking questions like, "What can I learn from this experience?" and "How can I use this experience to improve?" It's important to identify specific actions that can be taken to prevent the same mistake from happening again. For example, if the failure was due to lack of preparation, the lesson learned may be to devote more time to planning and preparation in the future.

Another key aspect of reframing failure as an opportunity for growth is to practice self-compassion. This means treating oneself with kindness and understanding, rather than harsh self-criticism. It's important to recognize that failure is a natural part of the learning process and that every failure provides an opportunity to learn and grow.

Finally, it's important to remember that reframing failure as an opportunity for growth is not a one-time event. It's an ongoing process that requires practice and commitment. By developing a growth mindset, focusing on the lessons learned, practicing self-compassion, and embracing failure as an opportunity for growth, individuals can develop the resilience and confidence needed to achieve success in any area of life.

Developing resilience and grit

Developing resilience and grit is essential for bouncing back from failure and achieving success in the face of adversity. Resilience is the ability to recover from setbacks, while grit is the perseverance and passion for long-term goals. Here are some strategies that individuals can use to develop resilience and grit:

a) Develop a growth mindset: A growth mindset involves seeing challenges as opportunities for growth and believing that failure is not a permanent state, but rather a temporary setback. This mindset helps individuals view failures as learning opportunities and become more resilient.

b) Set goals and pursue them with passion: Setting and pursuing goals with passion helps individuals develop grit, which is essential for achieving success in the face of adversity. It's important to have a clear vision of what you want to achieve and to remain focused and determined even when faced with obstacles.

c) Build a support network: Having a strong support network can help individuals develop resilience by providing emotional support and practical help when needed. This network can include family, friends, colleagues, mentors, and other like-minded individuals who share similar goals.

d) Practice self-care: Taking care of oneself is essential for building resilience and grit. This includes getting enough sleep, eating a healthy diet, exercising regularly, and engaging in activities that bring joy and fulfilment.

e) Embrace challenges: Embracing challenges is an essential part of building resilience and grit. Instead of avoiding difficult situations, it's important to approach them with a positive attitude and a willingness to learn and grow.

Developing resilience and grit is not an easy process, and it requires consistent effort and practice. However, by adopting a growth mindset, setting and pursuing goals with passion, building a support network, practicing self-care, and embracing challenges, individuals can develop the resilience and grit needed to overcome setbacks, achieve success, and thrive in any area of life.

V. Case Studies of Successful Business People Overcoming Obstacles and Coping with Failure

1. Oprah Winfrey: Oprah is one of the most successful media personalities of our time, but she faced many challenges in her life. She was born into poverty and endured abuse as a child, but she persevered and went on to become a successful talk show host, media executive, and philanthropist.

2. Steve Jobs: The late Steve Jobs co-founded Apple, a company that has revolutionized the technology industry. However, Jobs was also fired from his own company at one point and had to work hard to regain his position. He also struggled with health issues, but he remained dedicated to his work and continued to innovate until his death.

3. J.K. Rowling: The author of the Harry Potter series faced rejection from multiple publishers before her books finally became successful. She also dealt with depression and financial difficulties while writing her books, but she kept going and eventually became one of the best-selling authors of all time.

4. Elon Musk: Elon Musk is the founder and CEO of several successful companies, including Tesla and SpaceX. However, he faced many obstacles along the way, including multiple failed businesses and personal struggles. Despite these challenges, he remained committed to his vision and continued to innovate.

5. Colonel Sanders: The founder of KFC, Colonel Sanders, faced many failures before finding success. He started his chicken restaurant in his 60s and had to travel around the country to promote it. He also faced rejection from many potential franchisees before finally finding success with his recipe and brand.

6. Jack Ma: Jack Ma is the co-founder of Alibaba, one of the largest e-commerce companies in the world. He faced multiple rejections when he was looking for work after college, but he persevered and eventually started his own business. He also faced many challenges when he started Alibaba, but he remained committed to his vision and built the company into a global powerhouse.

7. Sara Blakely: Sara Blakely is the founder of Spanx, a company that revolutionized the shapewear industry. She faced multiple rejections from manufacturers when she was trying to create her product, but she eventually found a factory that was willing to work with her. She also faced challenges in the early days of her business, but she remained committed to her vision and built a successful company.

8. Richard Branson: Richard Branson is the founder of Virgin Group, a conglomerate of over 400 companies. He faced many failures early in his career, including a failed music company and a failed airline, but he continued to pursue his entrepreneurial dreams. He also faced personal challenges, including dyslexia, but he found ways to cope with these obstacles and achieve success.

9. Jeff Bezos: Jeff Bezos is the founder and CEO of Amazon, the world's largest online retailer. He faced many challenges in the early days of his business, including a lack of funding and technical issues, but he remained focused on his vision and persevered. He also faced personal challenges, including a divorce and health issues, but he continued to lead Amazon to greater success.

10.Mary Barra: Mary Barra is the CEO of General Motors, the first woman to lead a major global automaker. She faced many challenges when she first started working at GM, including a culture of complacency and a lack of innovation. She also faced personal challenges, including the death of her father when she was young, but she remained committed to her work and helped GM become more competitive and innovative.

These successful business people show that overcoming obstacles and coping with failure is a common theme among those who achieve great success. By staying committed to their vision, adapting to changing circumstances, and persevering through tough times, they were able to achieve their goals and inspire others to do the same.

Analysis of how they overcome those challenges

Here's an analysis of how some of the successful business people I mentioned earlier overcome their challenges:

a) Oprah Winfrey: Oprah overcame her difficult childhood by developing a strong work ethic and a sense of independence. She also pursued education and took advantage of opportunities to advance her career. In her professional life, she faced challenges such as being fired from her first job as a news anchor, but she persevered and went on to start her own talk show, which eventually became a media empire.

b) Steve Jobs: Steve Jobs overcame many challenges in his personal and professional life by staying true to his vision and constantly innovating. When he was fired from Apple, he founded another company, NeXT, which later merged with Apple, and he continued to push the limits of technology. He also faced health challenges, but he remained committed to his work until the end.

c) J.K. Rowling: J.K. Rowling overcame rejection and financial difficulties by staying focused on her writing and pursuing her passion. She also developed a strong support system of family and friends who encouraged her to keep going. She used her personal struggles and experiences to inspire her writing, and eventually, her books became some of the best-selling in history.

d) Jack Ma: Jack Ma overcame early failures and rejections by staying persistent and never giving up. He also embraced new technologies and opportunities, such as the internet, which helped him create Alibaba. He remained committed to his vision of connecting Chinese businesses with the global market and continued to innovate and expand his company.

e) Sara Blakely: Sara Blakely overcame manufacturing challenges by staying persistent and never giving up on her idea. She also relied on her own creativity and problem-solving skills to create a unique product. When she faced challenges in the early days of her business, she remained committed to her vision of empowering women and helping them feel confident in their own skin.

These successful business people all overcame their challenges by staying focused on their goals, developing a strong work ethic, and remaining committed to their vision. They also relied on their own creativity and problem-solving skills to find solutions to their challenges, and they never gave up on their dreams. By staying persistent and never giving up, they were able to overcome their obstacles and achieve great success.

Lessons Learned from their experiences

Here are some of the lessons that can be learned from the experiences of successful business people:

a) Perseverance: One of the key lessons that can be learned from successful business people is the importance of perseverance. Many of them faced significant challenges and setbacks along the way, but they never gave up. Instead, they stayed focused on their goals and kept pushing forward, even when things were difficult.

b) Innovation: Another lesson that can be learned from successful business people is the importance of innovation. They were able to achieve success by thinking creatively and coming up with new ideas and solutions to problems. They also embraced new technologies and opportunities that helped them to stay ahead of the competition.

c) Vision: Successful business people often have a clear vision for what they want to achieve. They remain committed to their goals and are willing to take risks in order to make their vision a reality. They also have a strong sense of purpose that helps them to stay focused and motivated.

d) Adaptability: Successful business people are also adaptable. They are able to adjust to changing circumstances and make the most of new opportunities. They are also able to learn from their mistakes and make changes to their approach when necessary.

e) Hard work: Finally, successful business people understand the importance of hard work. They are willing to put in the time and effort needed to achieve their goals. They also have a strong work ethic that helps them to stay focused and productive, even when they face obstacles or setbacks.

Common Mistakes to Avoid

Facing obstacles and failure is an inevitable part of running a business. However, how you respond to these challenges can make all the difference in the success of your business. Here are some common mistakes to avoid when facing obstacles or failure in business:

a) Giving up too soon: Many entrepreneurs give up at the first sign of failure or when they face an obstacle. It's essential to remember that success doesn't come overnight, and every business faces setbacks. Don't give up too soon and keep pushing forward.

b) Blaming others: It's easy to blame others when things don't go as planned, but taking responsibility for your actions is essential in business. You are in control of your business, so focus on what you can do to overcome the obstacle rather than blaming others.

c) Not learning from the experience: Every obstacle or failure is an opportunity to learn and grow. Take the time to reflect on what went wrong, what you could have done differently, and how you can prevent it from happening again in the future.

d) Focusing on the negative: It's easy to get caught up in the negative aspects of an obstacle or failure, but focusing on the positive can help you move forward. Look for the opportunities that come with the setback and use them to your advantage.

e) Losing sight of your goals: Obstacles and failures can be a distraction, but it's important not to lose sight of your goals. Stay focused on what you want to achieve and keep working towards it.

f) Not seeking help: Sometimes, it's necessary to seek help when facing an obstacle or failure. Don't be afraid to reach out to others for advice or support. A fresh perspective can help you see the situation from a different angle and come up with new solutions.

g) Trying to do it all alone: Building a successful business requires a team effort. Don't try to do it all alone, delegate tasks to your team members, and work together to overcome the obstacle.

By avoiding these common mistakes, you can better handle obstacles and failures in your business and come out stronger on the other side.

VI. The Impact of Obstacles and Failure on Business Success

Obstacles and failure are an inevitable part of running a business, and they can have a significant impact on its success. Overcoming obstacles and failure can build resilience and perseverance, two crucial traits for entrepreneurs that enable them to continue pursuing their goals despite setbacks. Additionally, obstacles and failure provide valuable learning experiences for entrepreneurs. By learning from their mistakes, they can make improvements to their business processes, products, or services. Furthermore, obstacles and failure can force entrepreneurs to think outside the box and come up with innovative solutions. This can lead to new products or services that can drive business success. Overcoming obstacles and failure can also require entrepreneurs to adapt to changing circumstances, such as a shift in the market or a change in customer needs, which is essential for business success in a constantly evolving business landscape.

Moreover, overcoming obstacles and failure can help entrepreneurs develop better decision-making skills. They can learn to make informed decisions based on their experiences and avoid repeating past mistakes. Additionally, overcoming obstacles and failure can improve teamwork among employees. Working together to overcome challenges can foster a sense of unity and collaboration, leading to a stronger team and ultimately a more successful business. In conclusion, while obstacles and failure can be challenging, they can also be an opportunity for growth and development. The key is for entrepreneurs to approach these challenges with a positive attitude and a willingness to learn and adapt. With the right mindset, obstacles and failure can be a catalyst for business success.

Importance of Adaptability in Overcoming Obstacles and Coping with Failure

Adaptability is a critical trait that can help individuals and businesses overcome obstacles and cope with failure. In today's fast-paced and constantly changing business environment, the ability to adapt to new situations and challenges is essential for success. An adaptable individual or business can embrace change and view it as an opportunity rather than a threat. They can quickly pivot their strategies and processes to meet new challenges and take advantage of emerging trends. This agility allows them to remain responsive to new opportunities and challenges and adjust their plans and strategies as circumstances change.

The ability to be flexible is another key aspect of adaptability. When an individual or business is adaptable, they can be flexible and adjust to new situations. This allows them to stay agile and quickly respond to any changes in the market or business environment. Being adaptable also means being resilient. Adaptable individuals and businesses are better able to bounce back from setbacks and continue moving forward towards their goals. They can learn from their mistakes and use that knowledge to improve their future performance.

Innovation is another crucial aspect of adaptability. Adaptable individuals and businesses are more likely to be innovative and find new ways of doing things. They are open to new ideas and are willing to take risks to achieve success. They can quickly and easily adapt to new technologies, processes, and market trends, ensuring that they remain competitive and relevant in their industry.

VII. Conclusion

Overcoming obstacles and coping with failure are critical skills for entrepreneurs and business leaders to develop. Throughout this chapter, we have explored various strategies and examples of individuals who have successfully navigated challenging circumstances to achieve success.

One key theme that emerged is the importance of maintaining a growth mindset, which involves embracing challenges and setbacks as opportunities for learning and growth. By reframing obstacles and failure in this way, entrepreneurs can remain positive, focused, and open to new solutions. Experimenting with different approaches, seeking out resources and support, and finding a mentor or advisor are all valuable strategies for overcoming obstacles.

Coping with failure requires resilience, grit, and the ability to learn from mistakes. Rather than becoming discouraged, successful entrepreneurs view failure as an opportunity for growth and innovation. By analyzing their mistakes and applying the lessons learned, they can avoid repeating the same errors and improve their chances of success.

In addition to these strategies, it is also important for entrepreneurs to avoid common mistakes such as failing to take responsibility for their mistakes, overreacting or becoming overwhelmed, giving up too soon, or failing to learn from their mistakes.

Ultimately, overcoming obstacles and coping with failure are essential skills for achieving business success. By developing a growth mindset, being adaptable, and cultivating resilience and grit, entrepreneurs can navigate the challenges of the business world with confidence and determination. While the journey may be difficult at times, with the right mindset and approach, entrepreneurs can turn obstacles and failures into opportunities for growth, innovation, and success.

Summary Of The Book

In this book, we've covered a wide range of topics related to developing a successful business mindset. We've explored the key characteristics of successful entrepreneurs, the importance of a growth mindset, and strategies for evaluating business ideas and opportunities. We've also delved into topics such as building a business plan, raising capital and financing your business, marketing and sales, managing your business, networking and collaboration, personal development, scaling and growth, overcoming obstacles and coping with failure, and future trends and innovation.

We've discussed the importance of having a proactive and positive attitude towards risk and failure, the power of persistence and perseverance, and the need for constant learning and adaptation. We've also emphasized the importance of self-awareness, emotional intelligence, and effective communication skills in building strong relationships and successful teams.

As you close this book, I encourage you to apply the principles and strategies discussed throughout these chapters in your own entrepreneurial journey. Remember that building a successful business takes time, effort, and perseverance, but with the right mindset and approach, you can achieve your goals and create a sustainable and fulfilling career.

Finally, I'd like to leave you with a few words of advice. First, stay focused on your long-term vision and goals, but be willing to adapt and pivot as needed. Second, never stop learning and growing, and seek out mentorship and guidance from those who have been where you are. And finally, embrace failure as an opportunity for growth and learning, and never give up on your dreams.

Thank you for reading, and I wish you all the best in your entrepreneurial journey

* 9 7 9 8 8 8 9 8 6 1 7 8 2 *